W9-CBB-960

DATE DUE

OCT 2 2 2009	
NOV 0 5 2009	
FEB 2 3 2011	
OCT 1 5 2012	
NOV 2 2 2012	
NOV 2 6 2012	
FEB 0 9 2015	
FEB 2 5 2015	
MAR 2 3 2015	
APR 2 0 2015	
MAY 0 9 2017	
AUG 1 4 2017	

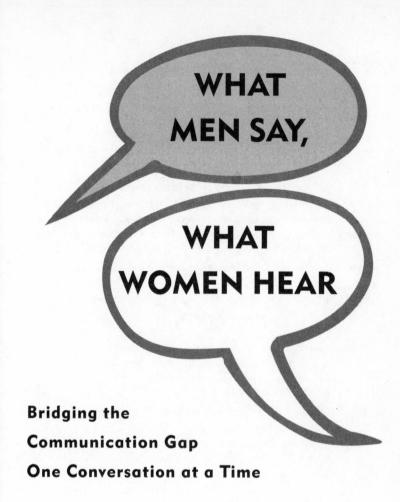

WHAT MEN SAY,

WHAT WOMEN HEAR

Bridging the
Communication Gap
One Conversation at a Time

DR. LINDA PAPADOPOULOS

Simon Spotlight Entertainment
New York London Toronto Sydney

Simon Spotlight Entertainment
A Division of Simon & Schuster, Inc.
1230 Avenue of the Americas
New York, NY 10020

First Simon Spotlight Entertainment hardcover edition January 2009

SIMON SPOTLIGHT ENTERTAINMENT and colophon are trademarks of
Simon & Schuster, Inc.

For information about special discounts for bulk purchases, please contact
Simon & Schuster Special Sales at 1-8000-456-6798 or
business@simonandschuster.com.

Designed by Diane Hobbing of Snap-Haus Graphics

Manufactured in the United States of America

10   9   8   7   6   5   4   3   2   1

Library of Congress Cataloging-in-Publication Data

Papadopoulos, Linda.
What men say, what women hear : bridging the communication gap one
conversation at a time / Linda Papadopoulos.
p. cm.
1. Man-woman relationships. I. Title.
HQ801.P295 2008
646.7'7—dc22   2008039071

ISBN-13: 978-1-4165-8521-3
ISBN-10: 1-4165-8521-4

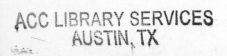

TO MY wonderful family—my parents for always making me feel safe, secure, and loved enough to face any challenge or go after any dream; my husband for making me laugh and letting me cry when I need it and making sure that I always feel there is someone looking out for me; and my amazing little daughter Jessica for helping me to see the world more beautifully and more clearly through her eyes.

ACKNOWLEDGMENTS

IT HAS taken a lot of input from several great people to bring this book to fruition: Paul Fedorko, Patrick Price, Michael Wilder, Alexandra Mizara, Amy Lawson. I feel a tremendous debt of gratitude to you all; thank you for believing in me and in this project. Thank you also to all those who read my books and take the time to share their thoughts and experiences with me, to those who believe in relationships and hope and love—this book would not have been possible without you nor would it have been worth writing.

CONTENTS

INTRODUCTION

Matt returns home after a bad day at the office. Rachel, his wife of five years, immediately corners him.

> RACHEL: Great, you're here. Now we can go through the fabric swatches I collected and pick one for the bedroom.

> MATT: For goodness sake, can't you even give me five minutes to take my coat off and relax? Plus, I thought we agreed the bedroom didn't need redecorating right away—we just did it two years ago.

> RACHEL: (*Matt doesn't love me enough or else he'd be more excited about the plans I'm making for our home. I want our house to be perfect for the both of us.*)

> MATT: (*I shouldn't have snapped but it felt like yet another demand, with a dig thrown in about how crappy our house looks. I can't do everything!*)

Sound familiar? This kind of scenario is played out in households all over the world, every day. Men and women talking to each other but misinterpreting what the other is saying—often with hurtful consequences.

It should be so easy. All those centuries of human development, socialization, and civilization have to count for something. We've sent men into space, women to the voting booths, and cloned a pretty impressive little sheep. Yet, when it comes to communication between the sexes, why does it feel like we're still at the "Me Tarzan, you Jane" stage?

How can "You look great!" end up being heard as "It's nice to see you make an effort—*for a change*"? Why does "I'll do the dishes after the football game" seamlessly transform into "I don't respect you enough to put effort into this relationship anymore"? And why do we even bother to ask the question "Does my butt look big in this?" when no answer on the face of the planet can ever be satisfactory?

Unfortunately for us social beings, there is a gulf in meaning between what we say and what others hear. This is true of any conversation but is particularly the case when it involves those we love, who we feel *should* understand us the most. But it is precisely in the context of personal relationships where we need to make the *most* effort to really understand each other and to acknowledge that to a large extent the way we interpret what is being said is based on the preexisting beliefs we hold about ourselves and the world around us, not always on the other's intent.

Miscommunication between the sexes is no real surprise. Society values each gender very differently, and this in turn plays a major part in how we communicate. Gender is a core factor that inevitably shapes not only how we respond to the world but also how the world responds to us. In the same way that we need to take into account the cultural norms of a person from a different country, we need to anticipate the cultural differences that will arise when a man and a woman try to understand each other. From car navigation to fashion to how many days you can safely leave leftover take-out Chinese food in the fridge before it becomes a health risk, there's likely to be little consensus between your average male and female. Mix in the weird and wonderful world of romance and *voilà*: opportunity for whole new levels of misunderstanding!

Of course, these healthy differences can work very effectively, as any woman who has ever flirted with a traffic cop to avoid getting a ticket can testify. However, the system often breaks down. Even simple compliments sound different once they've passed through our deep-rooted insecurities. Instead of accepting a compliment in the straightforward "Man Speak" in which it was meant, we choose to decipher it using our own "Woman Speak," and wires become crossed and messages confused. *What Men Say, What Women Hear* is designed to help you understand these messy man/woman transactions and guide you through the minefield that is romantic relationships. It's packed with tips to help ensure your relationship runs more smoothly, simply by having you learn to speak the same language. Because, as experience has taught me, this is the *only* path to true happiness in love.

Blissfully unaware of this simple truth, we try to address relationship problems in a million different and unsuccessful ways. We make unreasonable demands, we overpromise, we buy flowers and gift-wrapped boxes of chocolates to "say" we're sorry. But these strategies are useless because the underlying problem remains. It's impossible to tell somebody what he wants to hear when you can't understand what he's saying in the first place! It's difficult to read what is going on in a relationship when we're referring to only one translation guide—our own, gender-skewed version.

Fortunately, this doesn't require taking evening classes in male psychology. It's developing an *understanding* that every day of our lives we are socialized, one way or another, to speak and listen as a woman—not as a man. And there isn't a whole load of common ground between the two. Being aware of this is the first critical step toward harmony.

Once you've accepted this inextricable link between your biology and acculturation and their effect on how you react to and interpret the world around you (including your partner) then you will be able to really hear what is being said to you rather than merely responding to what you *expect* to hear. The key is perspective. Getting a grip on all these nonsensical yet strangely powerful thoughts comes down to establishing how realistic your current fears are and replacing them with a set of far more reasonable beliefs.

From initial attraction and early dates to meeting his family and the inevitable first fight, we'll use real-life scenarios to address communication trouble spots that can arise at significant milestones in a relationship. Often, the trick is as simple as accepting that "I'm busy tonight" doesn't mean "I'm too busy to have you in my life," or that "I love the blue dress on you" doesn't mean "I hate the red dress." Sometimes, it's a bit more complex and involves replacing deep-rooted thoughts and insecurities with a set of more sensible expectations. By addressing once and for all the double challenge of managing our own communication *and* comprehending our partners, *What Men Say, What Women Hear* will teach you how to develop a universal language, a common dialogue that you both understand. And while that doesn't mean he's suddenly going to respond, "Of course darling, I'm right on it!" the minute you ask him to remove his filthy laundry from the bedroom floor, it *does* mean that you'll learn to interpret his distracted grunt as just that, rather than an intentional insult that threatens the very fabric of your whole relationship. Likewise, once you begin to respond to what he is really saying rather than to what you *expect* him to say, he will unconsciously return the favor. It's called "modeling appropriate behavior" and basically means that if he feels that you are making a real effort to respect and understand what he is saying then it is very likely that he will return the favor. Eventually, discussing the laundry issue is not seen as an attempt to (a) run his life or (b) cage him into a boring domesticated relationship. And, with luck, he will learn that a quick "No worries, I'll do it now" is far easier in the long run. Stranger things have happened.

The beauty of acknowledging separate Man Speak and Woman Speak is that once we learn to understand each other and communicate fluently in each other's language then we can successfully create a generic dialect, which benefits both men and women. *What Men Say, What Women Hear* is your portable translation guide to every "He says, she says" relationship hurdle. You can't change the fact that men and women feel things differently. But you *can* establish a common language that allows you to identify, address, and work through these differences to secure your very own Happily Ever After.

CHAPTER 1

When He Says "Tomato," You Hear "I Hate You"

James and Anna are on a dinner date. The restaurant is cozy, the food delicious, and the conversation effortless. Everything is going very well, until James looks at his watch.

ANNA (*warily*): Going somewhere?

JAMES (*slightly bemused*): No, just checking the time.

ANNA: If you need to go . . .

JAMES: No, I really just wanted to see the time.

ANNA: Let's get the check. I need to be up early tomorrow.

JAMES: Are you sure? The caramel ice cream they serve here is out of this world.

Anna shakes her head. Exasperated, James pays the bill, and they drive home in uncomfortable silence, neither expecting to hear from the other again.

Who hasn't experienced something similar? Everything is going great and then in a flash the mood sinks. You can't quite put your finger on why, but you know what he is saying is not what you want to hear. And that's the thing about dating. Even though it's a great way to spend a Friday night, it also reveals the sometimes enormous gap between what is said by a man and what is heard by a woman and vice versa.

Yet, with a few simple tools, it's easy to crack the code and understand what the opposite sex really means. There are of course key differences in the way that men and women communicate, but both women and men are guilty of Common Thinking Errors (CTEs). These are irrational or erroneous beliefs that we hold about ourselves, another person, or a particular situation. Like when we make wrong assumptions about what other people are thinking and feeling, based on our past experiences. For example, your ex-boyfriend used to make fun of the size of your ankles, so when your new boyfriend praises you in jeans you might hear "You look great in jeans because they cover up those hideous ankles."

The point is that our thoughts are integral to the way that we relate to a situation emotionally. First we *think*, and then we have an emotional reaction based on that thought. Returning to the earlier example, when Anna saw James looking at his watch, she assumed he wanted to leave. Makes sense in her mind, since that was the way *she* got out of boring situations at parties: Look at your watch, say you're tired, and then excuse yourself. It never occurred to her that just because this was the way *she* did things it didn't necessarily mean that it was the way that her date did them. We're all guilty of this bias because making sense of the world means learning how to categorize like things. As babies we figure out that four-legged animals that go *woof* are all dogs. As women we figure out that two-legged mammals that wolf whistle as you walk by are all . . . you get the picture. We group things because it allows us to understand them more easily.

This strategy of remembering the past to help make decisions about the future does make sense in a lot of ways. Imagine eating a pretty red berry from the forest that promptly made you sick. It's important that you remember this in order to avoid being sick from red berries in the future. Now imagine a young, blond corporate lawyer with a southern drawl who broke your heart. Consciously or not you will begin to categorize features like "lawyer," "blond," and "southern drawl" to potentially mean things about other people and the way they will treat you. This type of irrational thinking extends not only to features of previous boyfriends but to messages that we received from others growing up. From your mom to the class bully, each and every one of your interactions will have to a lesser or greater degree affected the way you react toward the world around you. They're the origins and unwitting triggers of divisive Common Thinking Errors. Understanding and being able to contend with these CTEs is vital if you are going to be able to really hear and accurately interpret the words of others.

The first step in being able to tackle CTEs is being able to recognize them. Let's examine the six most common mistakes and remember that these errors are at the core of everything we discuss in the upcoming chapters:

1. All-or-nothing thinking. You think in complete extremes. *Either he tells me he loves me or our relationship is doomed* or *If he hasn't asked me on a second date by Tuesday, I'm never answering his calls again.* Now this is all very well and good, but the man in question doesn't have a copy of your rule book, so he has no idea that this is what you want. Who decided that this was the best criterion by which to judge a relationship? Where did your "rules" come from? He can't mind-read any more than you can, and thinking in extremes just creates ridiculously high expectations that no one can match. And usually only one person gets hurt by the outcome: you.

2. Maximizing the negatives. You only take notice of the downside of the situation. So what if he's the love of your life and he's reliable, handsome, and kind? He was standoffish with your mother last week and didn't want to go to your great-aunt's birthday party, so he must hate everyone in your life, and eventually he'll start to hate you too. The point is, if you are biased to see things in a negative way then you are much more likely to focus on the one negative point while ignoring everything else that would give you a more balanced view of the situation.

3. Making everything about you. You feel responsible for things that have nothing to do with you. *He's in a foul mood, it must be my fault. Clearly he's lost interest, and he's trying to push me away so that I'll back off and eventually finish it.*

Maybe he's in a foul mood because a coworker has messed up and now he'll have to spend the entire weekend sorting it out, when he'd rather be with you. Or perhaps he's tired and just feeling a bit under the weather. Whatever it is, it's important that you recognize that his world, his thoughts, and even his feelings may not always revolve around you. And even though it may upset you to see him down, many times the best thing that you can do is just give him the space to speak to you when he is ready and manage your own anxiety by remembering that his life is filled with a million and one things that have the potential to make him happy or sad. You are one of those things but by no means the only one.

4. Jumping to conclusions. You reach inaccurate conclusions based on insufficient or inadequate evidence. *He wants us to join a gym, which means he isn't attracted to me anymore. He thinks I've put on weight and let myself go. It's only a matter of time before he leaves.* Men tend to be much more straightforward than women. If he thought that, he would probably tell you. He wants to join a gym because, well, he does. He probably thinks it would be a good, fun way of keeping fit and a way for the two of you to spend more time together. If you immediately jump to conclusions, you never give yourself the chance to make sense of what is really going on. Also if you are going to sit around playing detective, it will eventually get tiresome for your mate. No one wants to be with someone who is constantly trying to unearth his hidden motives.

5. Seeing everything as a catastrophe. You focus on the worst-case scenario and exaggerate the likely consequences.

I've burned the romantic meal I planned for tonight. Every-thing's ruined and the evening will be a disaster. I don't like the dress I've bought either and he probably doesn't want to come here anyway. Slow down! Stop the spiral of doom in its tracks. Look at the facts. All that's happened is the chicken might be extra crispy. But the dessert looks fabulous, your hair is just the way you like it, and he is coming to see you, not the food. It all boils down to perspective. The more anxious you feel, the less perspective you are able to get on a situation. Take a minute to step back and really challenge those negative thoughts.

6. Generalizing the negatives. You exaggerate the memory of an unpleasant experience, which then affects other parts of your present life, even if they are entirely unrelated. A throwaway comment from your ex-boyfriend about how he's not really into blondes turns into *My hair looks bad, and if he thinks so, so will every other guy, and I'll end up dying a lonely old woman who never finds love!* Now, you know this isn't logical or reasonable thinking. Apart from anything else, "not being into blondes" is shallow, which is your ex's loss. There are millions of men out there with incredibly diverse tastes in women. Stop making huge generalizations about small, meaningless comments. He probably can't even re-member saying it!

Can you see how these thinking errors start to affect your behavior and, in turn, the way you live your life? One woman might sleep with every guy who takes her out for a drink be-cause she's established a false belief that sex is the only way to make a guy fall in love with her. Another woman might starve herself for a week before every date, because one guy told her she had "womanly curves." And, in an extreme example, someone may completely avoid dating altogether and close off the option of meeting anyone because she doesn't believe she deserves to find love. Each sounds ridiculous written down, but we're all guilty of this behavior in one form or another. With a few tweaks in the way we listen and interpret what we hear, we can radically change our lives for the better.

Common Thinking Errors don't appear overnight. They develop over years and stay with us, often unchallenged. And once ingrained, they become automatic. You don't even realize the havoc you are causing to your happiness. If you are going to have any chance of dissolving self-defeating CTEs, you must learn to reprogram those automatic negative thoughts with a more constructive strategy:

- **Identify it.** Thoughts give rise to emotions. *What am I feeling? Why am I feeling this way? What am I thinking about that is making me feel this way? What am I saying to myself?*

- **Dispute it.** *Is there an alternative way of seeing things? Am I unfairly biased? What evidence is there for the conclusion I reached?*

- **Tweak it.** *What would be an alternative way to make sense of things? Can I make my automatic negative thought more balanced? How much do I believe this alternative?*

- **Replace it.** *Do I feel better now that I am looking at things from a different perspective? Is this other way of looking at things at least a little realistic?*

- **Let it go.** *Am I ready to have some faith in challenging my established way of thinking? Will I let more rational and positive thoughts help me let go of my negative feelings?*

With this strategy, let's return one final time to the opening scenario with James and Anna. Everything was going so well over dinner until James looked at his watch. Let's try it again, but this time with Anna recognizing and challenging her CTEs and responding in a way that allows both her and James to really hear what the other is saying:

James looks at his watch.

ANNA: (*Is that a sign he wants to leave? Except we seem to be having a great time, so why would he want to leave? Maybe he is wondering what time it is.*) What time is it?

JAMES: Nearly midnight. I can't believe how time has flown. I'm having a great time.

ANNA: (*It's later than he thought, so maybe he does want to go. But he did say he's having a great time, as am I.*) Me, too. It's too bad we don't have another couple of hours.

JAMES: Well, there's always coffee. And this place has the best caramel ice cream you have ever tasted. We could also go out again next Friday night, if you're free.

ANNA: I'd love to. There's a film opening I really want to see.

JAMES: Great. It's a date.

It's amazing how differently things can turn out with a positive outlook. Instead of jumping to the negative conclusion that James was bored, she remained neutral. She **identified** that her feelings stemmed from the assumption that he wanted to leave because he looked at his watch. She **disputed** this assumption (*we seem to be having a great time, so why would he want to leave?*). She **tweaked** her line of thinking and **replaced** it with the idea that he *was* having a good time. She could then **let go** of her critical thinking error (he looked at his watch, he's bored, he wants to leave) and focus on what was really happening (he checked his watch and couldn't believe how time had flown!).

This allowed the evening to continue its course and gave James the opportunity to let Anna know how much he enjoyed being with her, without being too vulnerable. Anna had the encouragement from James to build on the idea that they wanted to see each other again, and hello, they've decided to pursue the relationship. And it all stemmed from Anna not imposing preconceived notions upon the simple act of checking the time.

New romantic relationships are remarkably fragile. Like any relationship, they take time to solidify and become dependable. Yes, right from the beginning of a relationship you can count on some awkward conversations, a lot of uncertainty, and a fair share of embarrassment experienced in equal amounts by everyone involved. The trick is to acknowledge that sometimes what we hear has a lot more to do with *the way we listen* rather than what is being said. We need to abolish the barrier that separates what we are experiencing from how we interpret that experience. It makes all the difference.

In the next chapter we'll examine how our perspective on the world influences our flirting techniques when we first meet someone we're attracted to—and how to make sure he gets the right message.

TIPS TO REMEMBER

- CTEs are inevitable, but you *can* change them.
- Get some perspective before getting upset.
- Pause before assuming you know what he is saying. Does he really mean that, or are you just interpreting his words based on past experiences?
- CTEs abound. Be aware of your thinking errors. They happen without you even realizing it.

CHAPTER 2

Flirting and Courting:
The Truth Behind "How Ya Doin'?"

Jennifer and Simon are in the library of the company where they work. Jennifer can't reach a book she needs on the top shelf and is looking around for help. Simon notices her.

SIMON: You're looking a bit lost. Can I help?

JENNIFER (*smiling broadly*): I need that large leather-bound book up there.

SIMON: No problem.

He reaches up and passes it to her.

JENNIFER: Thank you so much. Hurrah for tall, strong men! I don't know why they store these up that high.

SIMON: Seems a little silly. What department are you in?

JENNIFER: Marketing. You?

SIMON: Legal. Hey, any interest in grabbing a cup of coffee with me?

JENNIFER: Actually, I hear my in-tray calling me! I'd better go. But thanks.

SIMON: Oh. Okay. I don't suppose you're free for a drink sometime?

JENNIFER: I have a boyfriend.

SIMON: Oh, right. Sorry. See you around.

Okay, hands up everybody who thought that Jennifer was flirting with Simon. And who thought that Simon had completely misinterpreted Jennifer's signals?

A guy reading this would probably think that Jennifer was giving off flirty vibes. She smiled, described Simon as "tall" and "strong," and engaged him in more conversation than was strictly necessary. To Simon, it seemed natural to ask her out and confusing when she informed him she had a boyfriend. If you're a girl, however, you probably thought she was just being friendly, passing the time of day in a fun way, and rewarding him for helping her. Thus, Jennifer was taken aback by Simon asking her on a date. As far as she was concerned she was just acting in a friendly manner. And this is vital to understanding miscommunication between men and women when flirting.

Believe it or not, all of those cheesy one-liners you have to contend with on your Friday nights out aren't merely the annoying ramblings of inebriated, oversexed jerks. It turns out that they are actually a complicated system of social behaviors that we have developed throughout thousands of years of evolution. Every toss of the hair and lingering look received is part of a set of signals whose history and sophistication we are only now beginning to understand. Think of it like this: Flirting is nature's solution to the age-old problem faced by every animal species from emperor penguin to human—how to choose the best mate in a world that is teeming with possibilities.

When our species was young, we needed to evolve a way of quickly and safely figuring out the value of potential partners without having to connect too deeply or, for women, risk pregnancy with every possible mate encountered. And that is where flirting comes in. Flirting allows us to send and receive information about a potential mate, and even explore sexual chemistry safely and without much risk.

Research has shown that men nearly always perceive situations to be more sexually oriented than women. Men assume that behavior described by women as "just being friendly" is actually flirtatious and the other party is "interested." Women only have to smile at a man or accidentally catch his eye for most men to make the assumption that there is romantic potential on the horizon. With a lower threshold for interpreting "interested" behavior, men are far quicker to jump to the conclusion that something is likely to lead to a sexual/romantic liaison.

So why do these key differences occur? And what does it

actually mean for male-female communication in the potential minefield that is modern dating?

Flirting is much more than just a bit of fun. Anthropological research shows that flirting is found, in some form, in all cultures and societies around the world. It is a basic instinct, part of human nature, and with good reason. If we did not initiate contact with the opposite sex, we would not reproduce and humans would die out! Let's look at why flirting happens and how evolution, society, and popular culture have all shaped the way we flirt.

EVOLUTION

Time: 2:00 p.m.
Date: July 1, 30,000 BC
Location: Somewhere near a cave

Ugg and Trog are competing with each other for the attention of cavewoman Mog.

> UGG: I live near stream. I make fur skirt. We live in cave.
>
> TROG: I have good spear. I have big fire. We live on mountain.
>
> UGG: I kill Trog if he touch you.
>
> TROG: I kill Ugg if he touch you.
>
> MOG: Okay, look guys. I think you're both really cute and all, but I need a guy who's really in touch

with his feminine side and knows the meaning of emotional intimacy. I've just dated too many Neanderthals to get involved right now.

Perhaps it didn't go quite like that, but believe it or not, it's not too far from the truth of how flirting began. There are clear evolutionary reasons why men and women flirt, and these reasons go some way in explaining why men and women get their signals crossed in today's world. Now even though the whole point of flirting is to figure out if there is potential for mating, men's reasons for flirting are often different from women's. Sometimes, but not always, men simply want a sexual conquest. They are programmed to want to get it on with a girl, even if her flirting isn't overtly sexual. After all, evolutionary theory says that the whole point of life is to ensure that your genes are passed on. The more genes passed on, the better, since this will mean there is a greater chance more will survive. A man will make the reasonable assumption that it's better to try and fail than to not try and miss a reproductive opportunity altogether. So when he asks "How ya doin'" with a cheesy smile, he isn't being clumsy or heavy handed, he's simply reacting to thousands of years of biological hardwiring.

Women, however, nearly always flirt to engage in a relationship, not simply to have sex. This makes evolutionary sense, since unlike men, women can't spread their DNA around as easily. The fact that they get pregnant and historically have been responsible for childrearing means that they have to rely on *quality* (i.e., finding a guy who is not only good genetic material but will stick around and be a good father) rather than *quantity* (i.e., having as many sexual encounters as possible in the hopes of producing as many offspring as possible).

As such, a woman is instinctively programmed to be much more cautious and to underestimate a man's willingness to commit. She has far more to lose if she succumbs to flirting, sleeps with a man, and then is abandoned. Therefore, a woman is careful to whom she gives out sexual signals. She is more likely to be friendly and "see how it goes" rather than jump in and try to land a mate straightaway.

The things that attract men and women to each other have not changed a lot over the years. Throughout history and even to this day, men and women are valued for different qualities. Men are traditionally prized for their ability to hunt and gather (i.e., provide and achieve status in the group). Women, on the other hand, are valued for their youth and beauty, because this represents an ability to produce genetically desirable children.

When men started to live in groups, they needed to compete for resources including food, water, shelter, and the best females to give them strong offspring. The women, on the other hand, looked for the best providers, who could give them resources to live on, protect them, and also offer strong genes.

As intelligence in humans developed, brute force gave way to negotiation and competition for mates via flirting. Both sexes started taking notice of their appearance and grooming. The men tried to improve their status by getting the best shelter, food, and water supplies. The equivalent today would be a big house, a powerful car, and a job in an investment bank. Women tried to appear superfertile by wiggling their hips, reddening their lips, and tossing their hair.

In fact, women would compete with their own sex too, by showing off their clothing, growing their hair the longest, and comparing breast size. Today's equivalent would be perhaps expensive clothes, dieting to be the thinnest, and comparing breast size (nothing much changes!). Men would seek to have the most muscle, run the fastest, and kill the biggest deer. Today's equivalent would be . . . big muscles and running fast (I did say that not much changes!). Both evolutionary and social research show that men in most cultures look for women whose physical appearance demonstrates superfertility: large eyes, pouty lips, large breasts, and wide hips. Women are attracted to men who are clever providers—the strongest, the fastest runners, and the ones with an MBA need apply!

The fact that men and women are valued for different things means they will focus on different things when trying to attract each other's attention (i.e., flirt). For girls, it's going to be about investing in youth and beauty, and for guys, it's going to be about investing in a nicer car and higher status in society. Interestingly, research shows that women from all walks of life—from primitive agricultural societies to those who work on Wall Street—use nonverbal signals that are startlingly alike.

A woman who is flirting with a man will:

- Smile directly at him
- Make her eyes seem wider and more childlike by arching her brows

- Quickly lower her lids (once she is sure he has noticed her)
- Tuck her chin slightly down and coyly to the side and then exaggeratedly extend her neck, as a sign of vulnerability and submissiveness
- Avert her gaze, followed within seconds, almost on cue, by putting her hands on or near her mouth and giggling

For men it goes something like this:

- Place a palm up on the table or knees, so as to reassure the prospective partner that he intends no harm
- Laugh out loud to attract attention and to show dominance
- Extend a strong chin and show off muscles to confirm virility

By flirting in this manner he signals his ability to protect potential offspring as well as indicating that he has a softer side and will stick around, after the sex, for fatherhood.

Regardless of language or demographic factors, couples around the world tend to flirt in the same way. These universal gestures are very primitive behaviors driven by our brain's evolutionary memory. In fact, some comparative psychologists believe that a woman playing with her necklace while talking to a man is no different from a female wolf displaying submissiveness to a dominant male she's after.

Gives a whole new meaning to a wolf in sheep's clothing, don't you think?

Let's time-travel back to the present, to a high-octane party on New York's Upper East Side and witness the evolutionary process at work.

> KEVIN: That's the last time I trust Martin. I nearly lost my fifty-thousand-dollar bonus thanks to that idiot. Luckily I checked the figures myself. All I want to do is go back to my penthouse and relax in the sauna. Care to join me? My Ferrari is parked right out front.

> CLAIR: That would be wonderful. I hate going home in the dark on my own, especially in these heels, and I would love to see your place. Let me just thank Samantha for a great party.

Okay, so the dialogue is a little cheesy, but it illustrates the different ways that men and women are socialized into attracting a mate. There are nonverbal rituals as well. Clarissa will giggle, smile, gaze up at Kevin, sway on her heels, lick her lips, force her backside to tilt out and up, and push her breasts forward. She will be submissive and hugely exaggerate her sexuality. Kevin will swivel on his heels, arch his back, stretch to appear taller, and make flamboyant displays of clinking glasses with friends and laughing loudly. These exaggerated movements are not that different from some of the courtship displays engaged in by male gorillas. The point is to tell potential partners *Hey, look at me, I am strong and healthy, and even though I am really strong and powerful, I am not here to hurt you.*

All these displays were designed to bring the flirty pair to the touching part of the courtship: stroking, fondling, kissing, and eventually having sex. Of course, that is if everything goes according to plan. But that is not always the case. Because as everyone who has ever flirted knows, it can all go horribly wrong. That's often the case when the culprit "socialization" comes into play.

Beyond evolution, men and women are socialized into behaving in certain ways and consequently view relationships very differently. From the fairy tales that tell girls to be a submissive princess who waits for her knight to save her to the rough and tumble group sports that teach boys not to show emotion or weakness, we are constantly being molded into the gender stereotypes that guide the ways we understand and communicate with one another. It's no surprise therefore that women tend to be more creative, emotional, empathetic, and willing to share feelings, and men are more logical, analytical, rational, and geared to problem solving than emotional sharing.

Men operate on a physical and visual level. For them the way a woman looks is paramount when they first start flirting and dating. Many of the behavioral or social signals she gives off will be taken at face value. This means that many times he won't look at the bigger picture for subtleties or even try to interpret behavior within the context in which it is being exhibited. Thus, signals frequently get crossed.

If a pretty waitress at a restaurant is talkative and smiley toward a customer, laughs at his corny joke as she gives him his change, and continues to talk to him after she has delivered his order, he is likely to interpret that as sexual interest. Both from an evolutionary and a social perspective, that is what he is *programmed* to do.

Now this is where things can get tricky. If he responds to the waitress's friendliness by indicating his sexual interest, it will at best end with embarrassment on both sides and at worst with him wearing part of his second course. From the waitress's point of view, she was just doing her job. After all, being friendly means better service, which means a better tip. In his mind, though, he saw a pretty woman, a sexual being, who was giving off signals that showed high levels of interest. In most cases, other factors, such as the setting, the hierarchical context of their relationship (i.e., it's her job to serve him), the fact that she was just as friendly and chatty to the old lady at the next table, may register but not as highly as the fact that she has good DNA and she is *flirting*.

As you can see, the whole realm of flirty communication is studded with pitfalls. Men are more, shall we say, meat and potatoes about the whole thing. They will flirt and talk to women because they want sex. Women tend to approach the whole process a bit more methodically; they will usually flirt and show interest in men when they feel there is potential for a relationship. This explains how and perhaps why flirting signals are often manipulated to give a person the best chance that the object of his or her desire reciprocates his or her advances. Men will often give "commitment" signals while flirting in order to have sex. And women may give off "flirty sex" signals to buy more time to figure out if the man is relationship material or not. It can seem as if nature is playing a very cruel trick on humans, making the sexes speak different languages to achieve very different aims.

Given the potential for all those pitfalls, how can you make sure you flirt without misunderstanding or being misunderstood? According to body language experts, there are six secret sexual signals that will tell you someone is flirting with you and help you decipher flirty body language.

1. The flirty pyramid. We focus on different parts of the body and face depending on whom we are meeting and how we feel about him or her. In a business-type situation, we generally look from eye to eye and across the bridge of the nose. With friends, our focus drops below eye level and moves into a triangle shape to include the nose and mouth. But once we start flirting, the triangle gets even bigger, widening at the bottom to include the entire body.

2. Lip reading. As the flirting gets more intense, the flirter's gaze will focus on the mouth as if he is trying to imagine kissing you. It may seem obvious, but most times it's our subconscious that picks up this sensual signal.

3. Subliminal eyebrows. When we see someone who we like, our eyebrows rise and fall very quickly. It lasts only about one fifth of a second. And if he too is attracted, he will do the same. Now because it happens so fast it's not an easy one to pick up. Keep a lookout for this sign, though, as scientists have found that the gesture is replicated in every human culture. If you want to make it clear that you like someone, try prolonging your eyebrow flash for a whole second. He won't know what hit him.

4. Love compass. Now this is an interesting one. Next time you are in a room full of potential dates and you can't decide whom to focus on, just take a look at your feet and hands. We tend to point our limbs toward the person we're interested in. If we find someone attractive, we'll often point at him subconsciously. And just as we are unaware we are doing this, the person at whom your toes or arms are pointing will be aware that you are showing interest. They just won't be sure why.

5. Playing mirror mirror. This involves copying what the other person is doing. If he leans forward, you lean forward. If he looks you in the eye and smiles, you do the same. Nothing bonds two people more than mirroring behavior. The reason that it works is based on the premise that we like people who are like us. When someone acts the way we do, we are more inclined to think that he is like us in deeper ways, too.

6. Blinking. When we find someone attractive our pupil size increases and we begin to blink at a faster rate (à la Betty Boop). If you want to check out whether someone reciprocates the attraction that you feel, try increasing the blink rate of the person you're talking to by blinking more yourself. If the person likes you, he'll unconsciously try to match your blink rate to keep up, which in turn makes you both feel more attracted to each other!

As with most things to do with flirting, it's important to take into account the big picture so you have a better chance of being clear about what is being said. Make sure that you don't judge on one thing alone. Instead, look for clusters of behaviors. Experts suggest that to be confident about your body language decoding skills you need to look for at least four signals that say the same thing before you can be confident about what your eyes are telling you. Flirting is a great first step in the quest to find Mr. or Ms. Right, and although we can trust our animal instincts to an extent, when we start dating and have to use our powers of rationality and logic, things can get *really* confusing.

TIPS TO REMEMBER

- The flirtation stage of a relationship can be scary and confusing; look for signs.
- Be aware of what signals your body is sending out.
- Pay attention to what you say and how you say it. Innocent comments give off different signals, depending on the gender of the person hearing them.

CHAPTER 3

The Fun and Frustrating First Dates

Tom and Jodie have just finished their first date. They are parked in front of her apartment building after a night of dinner, drinks, laughter, and great conversation. They linger in the car, delaying the end to a great night.

> TOM: I wish this night would never end.

> JODIE: So do I.

Jodie smiles at Tom. Tom smiles back.

> TOM: I really had a great time, should I call you?

> JODIE (*after a noticeable pause*): Sure. Whatever. Thanks for tonight. See you soon.

They never speak again.

How many first dates can you recall that disappointedly ended this way? You both had a great time, enjoyed each other's company, only for it to amount to nothing when you never hear from each other again. What happened?

Jodie and Tom have been attracted to each other for months. Friends of friends, they spent hours asking far-from-subtle questions such as "Can he cook?" "Does she like basketball?" and "Please, please, please tell me you've invited her to your birthday party." They've even not so casually inquired about the other's relationship history. And finally, after *months* of agonizing over whether "just passing by" someone's place of work is cute or creepy, and obtaining each other's phone numbers via a cryptic chain of friends, they go on a date.

And it's a success! She thinks he is funny. He admires her beauty. He loves her sweet nature. She finds him generous. In short, the beautiful flowers, swanky restaurant, and ridiculously good wine provide the perfect backdrop for the most romantic date of their dreams.

So, what happened? How did their magical night mutate into a date from hell? Because what they *said* didn't reflect what they were really feeling. Let's replay Tom and Jodie's scene and take a look at their *inner* dialogue to uncover where the communication lines broke down.

> TOM: I wish this night would never end. (*This was wonderful. We really connected!*)
>
> JODIE: So do I. (*It doesn't have to.*)

Jodie smiles at Tom. Tom smiles back.

TOM: (*She's brilliant. I definitely want to see her again. But I don't want her to think I'm rushing things so I won't suggest coffee.*)

JODIE: (*He's amazing! I hope he wants to come in for coffee. I don't want the night to end.*)

TOM: I had a great time. Should I call you?

JODIE: (*He doesn't even want to come in! I just said I didn't want the night to end and I smiled at him. And then he used the "I'll call you" line. If he's not into me, then I won't be into him.*) Sure, whatever. Thanks for tonight. See you soon.

TOM: (*Whatever?! Whatever?! What happened? I thought she liked me as much as I liked her. How could I misread the situation so completely? Well, I'm not going to humiliate myself by pushing the issue.*)

Awkward silence.

JODIE: (*He hasn't even tried to kiss me or mention a second date. This evening was a total bust.*)

They never see each other again.

See what happened? Jodie and Tom let their perceptions cloud the other person's actual intent. The promising night ended disappointingly because of their individual insecurities and inhibitions and their inability to convey what they were thinking and what they wanted. There were too many missed signals and overlooked opportunities. In trying to act casual and not appear overly eager, they completely misunderstood each other. Welcome to the potentially explosive minefield known as the First Date.

If only it were simple! You find each other attractive and interesting and slip into a healthy, mutual relationship. Wouldn't that be the grown-up thing to do? Unfortunately, love will never be as easy as it could be. From the moment you are born, the world you grow up in and the experiences you encounter color your perceptions. And this can have dramatic and profound effects long after you become an adult and leave the family home. Your early experiences can fix your mind-set so you always interpret certain signals in a negative way—despite evidence to the contrary. An example of this could be always hearing "I'd like to see you again" as "I don't really like you, but I'm trying to be polite." Putting a negative spin on what a guy says or always expecting the worst can be the difference between succeeding or failing at relationships.

For example, when Stephanie is on a date, she filters any new information through her fixed mind-set of inadequacy. Even if her date tells her, "I had a fantastic time tonight," instead of accepting and enjoying the compliment, she'll interpret it as *He's only being nice because he doesn't know me or just wants to sleep with me. What a jerk!* Meanwhile, Ray, after months of deliberation, finally summons the courage to ask the object of his interest to dinner. She agrees and all goes well until she mentions that next time they should catch a movie. Ray interprets this as *She probably hated the restaurant I chose tonight, so she wants to avoid such a disastrous evening on our next date.* Ray then stumbles his way through a dejected good-bye speech before ushering his date out of the car before she even has a chance to hang around with glazed eyes doing the whole first date *Will we? Won't we?* kiss thing. Thus, your own fixed mind-set can have far more influence than the original meaning. In fact, the original meaning is lost, because your fixed mind-set is so powerful.

The key point to remember is that we all have history. And every time you initiate a new romantic relationship and go on a first date, your previous experience in similar situations comes into play. And so does your potential partner's. You have to learn to negotiate the muddy waters. In the twenty-first-century Western world, dating has become the primary form of meeting a life partner. In fact, it has become a crucial hurdle that almost every relationship must survive in the transition from platonic to romantic.

Men see dating very differently from women, which means the first date will be experienced differently, too. The pace of the initial stages will be perceived differently, and ultimately, the reality of being part of a couple will be felt differently. Once you accept this, you're halfway there.

Another issue that can affect first dates is who should take the lead. Despite decades of feminism and equality, the latest research indicates that women still want men to make the first move. Forget the "Go get him" girl-power messages churned out by shows such as *Sex and the City*. It seems we're secretly all still waiting to be asked out. And, according to studies, if a woman does ask a guy out, she's likely to be seen as a "nonserious dater" and more sexually active or permissive than a woman who was asked out by a guy.

In other words, once women begin to adopt certain "male"

dating traits, such as initiating a date, they are also assumed to have adopted other traditionally male objectives, i.e., noncommitment sex. The majority of guys in one study also reported that they had higher expectations for sex on a date when a woman asks them out than vice versa. Interestingly, men who were asked out on a date by a woman ended up having sex *less* frequently than did the guys who asked a woman out. Sorry guys!

But while most women want men to make the first move, a shift in society's expectations means that many guys are unsure what to do. The confusion about sexual stereotypes also may become evident in other ways on a first date now that the rule books have changed in terms of who pays, who opens the door, and who invites whom back for a nightcap. It's understandably confusing stuff!

What *is* consistent is that men and women are looking for the same qualities in a mate that they've always been looking for: a sense of humor, a kind nature, an ability to meet each other's emotional and physical needs. The problem isn't that men and women are seeking vastly different things. The problem is that their seeking methods are very different.

But don't give up hope and avoid dating entirely. The more you recognize what is going on and why it's happening, the easier it will be for you to control your dating life. Understanding the key factors at work during these loaded encounters will go a long way toward making everything go as smoothly and as successfully as possible and help you skirt disaster.

BE CLEAR ON BOUNDARIES

Christopher waits for Abigail outside a restaurant, where they are meeting for their first date. Abigail comes running up.

> ABIGAIL: I am so sorry. Have you been waiting long? I lost my apartment keys, then the traffic was awful. I thought I'd never get here . . .

> CHRISTOPHER: At fifteen minutes past our reservation and no word from you, I was getting a little worried.

> ABIGAIL: I am so sorry! I forgot my cell so I couldn't call.

> CHRISTOPHER: Well, I'm glad you made it. With any luck, the restaurant held our table. If not, we can always fill up on popcorn and hot dogs at the movie.

> ABIGAIL: Sounds like a plan.

This might be their first date, but already, Christopher gave Abigail a subtle clue about one of his pet peeves—he doesn't like people being late. It might not seem important, but everyone has particular codes of behavior that are important to them. Thus it's smart to set them out from the beginning, in a clear but friendly way, so there are no misunderstandings. Even though the first date is where both parties are trying to be on their best behavior, it is also where the boundaries of any potential relationship are set up. Each of you will pick up on clues about the other that will help you start to get a sense of each other's beliefs and values.

It's important to be aware of how you set these boundaries. If it's something you feel strongly about, like not having sex on a first date, then be explicit and tell him the rules. If, on the other hand, you have a thing about punctuality, you can afford to be a bit gentler about how you approach the matter and convey the message more subtly. Being a bit late for a first date is not the end of the world. If the relationship continues and it becomes a problematic pattern, you'll have plenty of time to tackle it then.

Boundaries are areas open for wild misinterpretation. For instance, Deb doesn't really like staying out past midnight on a weeknight because she knows she struggles to get up in the mornings. Instead of telling Rick why, she just insisted on being home at a certain time. For the first few dates, Rick interpreted this as Deb being bored with his company! It's important that you're always clear in your message. Having said that, don't go too heavy on the message either. Not that you would show up on your first date with a clipboard and red pen ready to list your personal boundaries, including no kissing without flossing first, flowers on every date, and no sex until the marriage proposal! Subtlety is important. Phrases such as "It would be really great if we could . . ." or "I really feel that . . ." rather than "You should/must/have to . . ." work best. But *do* speak up. If you're not happy about something—say, the fact that he never calls you when he says he will, or he always chooses where you go on dates— it will grow into something huge by the sixth date and be much harder to tackle then without resentment.

Interestingly, people with similar personal boundaries are more likely to date each other over the long term. So it's important to stick to your boundaries when you date—it might just ensure you find the man of your dreams.

BE AWARE OF THE POWER STRUGGLE

Greg picks up Tiffany for their first date, but they have a little time to kill before their dinner reservations.

> GREG: Do you want to get a quick drink before dinner? I know a great little bar just around the corner.
>
> TIFFANY: Suki's? I'm not a big fan of their wine. We *could* try this little Moroccan place that just opened. It's really cool and they do really cute little aperitifs.
>
> GREG: Sure, if you prefer. It's just that Suki's is so laid back. It would give us a chance to talk. I'm also a regular, so I know we would get great service.
>
> TIFFANY: True. But don't you want to be adventurous and try a new place?
>
> GREG: Yeah, you're right. Let's give your place a shot.

This might look like an innocent chat about their preferred drinking establishments, but actually both Greg and

Tiffany are (consciously or not) struggling to get the upper hand in this little exchange. They both want to demonstrate that they're in control of the situation, that they decide the agenda, and that they can influence the other person with their knowledge and/or status. Believe it or not, who holds the power in a relationship is often established very early on. Couples often dance back and forth verbally, testing their powers, watching for reactions and areas of weakness and strength in order to play their best hand. Sound cynical? It's not as dog-eat-dog as it appears. It's simply a mechanism to establish how the relationship will work, who will make the decisions, who will lead, and who will determine, ultimately, whether the relationship continues. A lot of people view having the power in the relationship as a means of having control over how it progresses. The belief is that the more power you have, the less likely you are to get hurt if the relationship fails.

Like any great partnership, the key to a healthy relationship is to have both parties feel empowered and safe enough to assert their views and beliefs. However, because first dates are all about testing new waters and figuring out who the other person is—or, more importantly, who they *want to be* in the relationship—most people are very wary of giving up too much power too soon. This is why both parties tend to be anxious about seeming too interested in the other too quickly. Which is why Tom, in this chapter's opening scenario, didn't push Jodie for a second date and why Jodie replied to Tom's asking if he should call with "whatever." Both feared, as all of us do, that by showing our true feelings, we're relinquishing power. Of course the truth is that you are going to have to find some way of signaling interest if you want that first date to lead to a second. If you don't want to commit verbally, it's time to reengage your flirting skills! A lingering look lets a guy know you're interested without you having to put yourself on the line by explicitly spelling out your feelings. The point is to appear confident, not arrogant, and to keep in mind that the only way forward is to share both the power and the responsibility of the relationship.

GATHER ALL THE DATA YOU CAN

Greg and Tiffany are now having a great time at dinner. Tiffany asks Greg what he likes to do for fun in his neighborhood.

> GREG: It must have been about five years ago that I went down to this bar, Liquids, near my apartment. This amazing live band was playing. Who knew I would be hooked on salsa music ever since!

> TIFFANY: Really? I love Cuban music! I don't know many of the bands but I really got into it during a visit there.

> GREG: You went to Cuba? My father was born there but I've never been. I always wanted to go!

> TIFFANY: You're close to your parents then? Are they still married?

GREG: Thirty years and counting.

TIFFANY: My parents have just celebrated their thirty-fifth. Can you imagine being married that long?

The exchange above may seem like an innocuous bit of chitchat, but there is a whole lot more going on below the surface. Tiffany and Greg are both on a mutual fact-finding mission. He wants to see if their music tastes are compatible. She wants to know if his parents have a happy marriage so she can see if he's had a good relationship role model. These two different agendas are typical; men tend to be interested in practical information, women in the more emotional stuff. Tiffany and Greg are also both ready to divulge lots of personal information about their tastes and their backgrounds, in an attempt to find common bonds. As well as discreetly letting each other know if you're interested in continuing the romance and finding out whether you both feel the same way, first dates have a lot to do with information gathering. What's this person all about?

Remember evolution's role in flirting? When evolution teams up with all those messages that we get from the society we live in, it results in behavior that scientists explain with what they call "social matching theory" or the "similarity principle." The theory states that people tend to fall in love with those who are similar to themselves. We're attracted to people who share the same opinions, interests, values, and experience. So much of a first date is flushing out *How like me is my date?*

But we're not after a cloned version of ourselves, and looking for some differences is healthy. Studies show we subconsciously tend to look for people who *complete us* (forgive the *Jerry Maguire* reference), making up for qualities we might lack. For example, if we are not very good at standing up for ourselves, we may see our partner's assertiveness as very attractive. The reason we frantically gather information on a first date is to work out how alike (or not) we are and if we will complement each other.

REALIZE YOU HAVE THE SAME GOAL

Greg and Tiffany's date is at an end. They stand outside her apartment building after a successful and fun night.

TIFFANY: I've had a wonderful time. I hope you understand if I don't invite you in for coffee.

GREG: That's cool with me. I would prefer to take things slowly. I had a good time too and would really like to see you again.

TIFFANY: Great! And don't forget, I'd love to hear those Cuban music CDs you mentioned. Here's my e-mail address. Send me some of the names.

GREG: Definitely. And I'll suggest some dates when we can get together. Maybe we should try a Cuban bar next?

Success! Tiffany was terrified that after such a successful first date, Greg would automatically expect they were going to have sex. She was pleasantly surprised when he agreed it wasn't a good idea and that he didn't like rushing into physical relationships either. It turned out that their goals were much closer than either had anticipated. Better still, they managed to use the interaction to confirm they'd had a good time and wanted to see each other again.

We often assume that our date has one expectation when the opposite is often true, and it's something that can prevent a relationship getting off the ground. While there is no getting away from the fact that men and women are very different in how they approach romance, the stereotype of a man just wanting sex on every first date is a myth. As is the desperate woman who wants to drag her date down the aisle and force him into having babies before he's even finished his dessert. Contrary to common opinion, men enter a relationship with the desire to fall in love more often than women do, and they fall in love more quickly. Consequently, although it may result in them being called commitment phobic, men are less willing to marry without being sure they are in love. As human beings we're programmed to want to connect and bond with the opposite sex in a meaningful way. Chances are both you and your date are hoping this could be the start of something special.

BE A DATER, NOT A DATEE

The way to overcome your negative mind-set caused by previous bad relationships or gender expectations that men should always do the chasing is to challenge them. Why assume a blatant compliment is a veiled insult? What evidence do you have for this? Why should you wait for him to call, just because your mom always told you that "only loose women make the first move"? Learn to be active in the process. Be a part of it. Don't wait for it to happen to you. And enjoy it. Our culture of fast food, instant results, and Botox treatments during our lunch breaks means we expect high-speed connections in *all* areas of our life. It's easy to start expecting a ready-made relationship, but the reason many relationships fail is because one or both parties judge the pace incorrectly.

New relationships are remarkably fragile. They take time to solidify and become dependable. Take it slow and stop worrying about results. You won't enjoy the race if all you can think about is the finish line. First dates in particular carry an enormous sense of expectation around them. Forget worrying where the first date will take you. Instead, use that energy to embrace and enjoy it. Who cares if he wants kids and you don't when you haven't even ordered dessert? The goal is to challenge preconceptions and expectations, understand the difference between how men and women view dating, and above all learn to accept that although dating is often a fraught and anxious activity, it can also be great fun.

TIPS TO REMEMBER

- Be assertive. Forget societal expectations that discourage you from taking the initiative. Make the first move if you want to!
- Say what you mean. Don't hold back because you're afraid being excited to see him again will put him off. If he likes you, he'll be thrilled and relieved by your honesty. If it scares him off, he wasn't right for you from the start.
- Forget past hurts or bad relationships. "All men are the same"–type thinking is destructive. Treat every romantic encounter as a fresh, exciting experience.
- Learn to enjoy the first dates and don't try to rush them into ready-made relationships.

CHAPTER 4

Welcome to Coupledom

Paul and Stacie have dated for three months. The relationship is entering the couple stage, and while things are going well, Stacie has voiced her concerns about their level of intimacy. Paul calls Stacie to plan their weekend.

> PAUL: Why don't we go hiking this weekend, just the two of us?

> STACIE: You know I love our hikes, but we never get to *talk*.

> PAUL: We can talk as we walk.

> STACIE: No, we can't. You walk too fast and I end up trailing behind, watching your cute butt all day. It's a pretty sight but a bit boring after a while.

> PAUL: I'll walk slower.

STACIE: I knew you would say that. Can't we just
do something else?

If you think this little scenario is just about Stacie hating
hiking, look a little closer. The happiest couples in the world
are those who understand and empathize with each other's
feelings and point of view. It is hard to elevate a new relationship to boyfriend/girlfriend status if there is a lack of
emotional intimacy. Men and women express closeness and
emotional intimacy in very different ways, and that's where
communication can really break down. But what constitutes
intimacy and how is it achieved?

WHAT INTIMACY MEANS

Intimacy means sharing emotional experiences together. It
involves a willingness to trust and commit yourself within
the relationship. In order to be truly intimate, you must also
be willing to be vulnerable. Interestingly, unlike sex, reason-
ably priced shoes, and the importance of baseball, when it
comes to intimacy, men and women agree on what intimacy
means and both appear to want the same thing. As per usual,
they just have different ways of obtaining it.

Women are far more inclined than men to get emotionally attached quickly. All it takes for many women is one
date and she's already trying to work out what her future
children's names will be and whether the flowers in her
bridal bouquet should match her husband-to-be's eyes.
They like the idea of settling down and its inherent exclusiv-
ity and commitment.

Men like variety. They're far more into the idea of dating lots of women. Remember, men have that evolutionary need to spread their genes around, and thus they need to explore their options. Men are all about options. While a woman may view a quick drink after work as one step closer to the jeweler, to him it might be just that—a quick drink.

The differences in thought process between men and women at this stage of dating can be quite noticeable. Just the way they interpret how a relationship is progressing can be quite telling.

Jane and Rob have been dating for several months, exclusively. Jane breaks down last night's date with her best friend, excitedly replaying the details as she remembers them.

JANE: So then he takes my hand and says, "Janey, you're so beautiful. I can't believe you want to be with me."

LARA: Oh my god, that's nearly a proposal.

JANE: I know, I know. I'm so excited! Lara, I really think Steve's *the one*. I mean, I think we could move in together soon.

LARA: But whose apartment will you choose?

JANE: I would think mine. It's got an extra bedroom and two bathrooms . . . although his does have that terrific view. This is so amazing.

LARA: You're so lucky. For fun, let's go look at some bridal gowns online.

Meanwhile, Steve discusses his view of the same relationship with his roommate.

ROB: Good time last night?

STEVE: Yeah. We ate at that new pizza place and then went to a movie.

ROB: You two are seeing a lot of each other. You really like her?

STEVE: She's great. I don't want to rush things, though. We're just having a good time.

ROB: Right with you there, buddy. Take it nice and slow.

STEVE: That's what's cool about Jane. She's really laid back. There's no pressure like with some girls.

ROB: Lucky for you.

How can two people have such completely different takes on the same evening? It's all down to interpretation. She's hearing something very different from what he's actually saying. In general, women talk more about intimate issues such as feelings and insecurities. Men look for similar interests, place more emphasis on undertaking joint activities, and typically avoid discussing feelings. Look at the two different breakdowns of the same date. The women discuss the emotional elements, a proposal, the future, and moving in together, while the men are content to accept the easygoing status quo.

This illustrates the differences between the two genders. If you introduce two women, it's likely that within the first hour (if not sooner) they will have moved on to "relationship talk," swapping experiences or comparing notes from their personal lives. Two men, however, are far more likely to identify immediately what football teams they support or what gym they attend. They stick to the safe neutral ground of common interests, without straying near any messy emotional stuff. Thus, the two genders are unprepared to communicate with each other. Jane is *hearing* from a woman's perspective but Steve is *talking* from a man's perspective. Neither realizes that their translations are totally out of whack.

Simply put, men apply different criteria for intimacy. Whereas a group of women can dissect and analyze a world-threatening dilemma such as "Does my boss hate me?" "Can I wear this dress with those shoes?" or "Will I ever find the one?" for hours on end, men simply prefer, the majority of the time, not to talk about it. It's a fact of life. If your idea of a great first date is to detail exactly what went wrong in former relationships and the effect it had on your poor crippled heart, don't expect him to reciprocate. A man would rather move on and *do something* than sit around and analyze it, whatever "it" may be.

Returning to Paul and Stacie's hiking conversation, let's delve into the subtext. Stacie has complained before that she doesn't feel close to Paul. Paul has gone away to think about this and he came up with the hiking idea.

> PAUL: Why don't we go hiking this weekend, just the two of us? (*When we go hiking, I feel really close to you.*)

STACIE: You know I love our hikes, but we never get to *talk*. (*I don't want to hike right now. I want to discuss how serious our relationship is.*)

PAUL: We can talk as we walk. (*I love spending alone time with you. I wouldn't take you hiking if I wasn't serious about you.*)

STACIE: No, we can't. You walk too fast and I end up trailing behind, watching your cute butt all day. It's a pretty sight but a bit boring after a while. (*This is your way to avoid talking about our relationship.*)

PAUL: I'll walk slower. (*Why are you being difficult? This is normally something we love to do.*)

STACIE: I knew you would say that. Can't we just do something else? (*You aren't taking my needs seriously. If you don't take me out to dinner, it means you don't really want to spend time with me.*)

Both Paul and Stacie want to connect and take the relationship to the next level, but they have different methods of expressing intimacy. For Paul sharing a favorite activity with the woman he loves is the perfect way to spend time together. He feels that sharing an adventure is the route to growing closer. On the other hand, Stacie feels that to grow closer *emotionally*, they actually need to talk about emotions. Neither party is right or wrong; they just approach the situation in their own gender-specific ways.

What differentiates romantic relationships from the other

bonds in our lives is how much of ourselves we share. Aside from sharing ourselves physically with a boyfriend or girl-friend, we often spend more time with a romantic partner than with family or friends. And in a healthy, happy relation-ship, we feel free to share our inner feelings with a part-ner in a way that would be unusual in a family or platonic relationship. Sharing things with our partner we wouldn't share with anyone else is one of the great things that make relationships so special, but for many people, it's also the hardest thing to do.

We've all been out with men who came on strong at first, then withdrew the minute feelings were mentioned. As we've discussed, since women are more apt to communicate feelings and prefer to talk about issues and people close to their hearts, they bond with friends by sharing experiences and stories. And when it comes to sex, emotional bonds play an important part in a woman's responsiveness and satisfac-tion. It is this connection that is actually one of the biggest physical turn-ons for women. Hearing why a man loves her and why she is special to him has the potential to be as sexually seductive as perfect six-pack abs. For a woman, being told that she is beautiful, funny, and clever is a huge aphrodisiac, especially if she's told that by a man whom she respects—she can then judge the compliment to be genu-ine. Emotional intimacy both in and out of the bedroom is the cornerstone of what a relationship means to a woman.

For men the link is more biological. Being "left-brain-competent," they often gravitate toward fields such as math, physics, and engineering and tend to prefer shar-ing activities and interests rather than feelings as a means of achieving intimacy. This doesn't mean he finds a feisty bout of quantum physics sexy, it just means that he is more comfortable discussing practical things, such as the gym and work, than his deepest, darkest insecurities. Men are less open to talking about emotions and less responsive to attempts by women to change this behavior. It is just how his brain is programmed. To complicate things further, men don't find the need to reinforce the intimacy they feel in relationships all that often, and they assume that this is also true for their partner. The age-old adage of "But you know I love you, honey, why do I need to keep telling ya?" comes from this core male/female difference.

Most women need and want more than just sporadic acts of intimacy if they are going to feel truly connected in the relationship. They desire sustained feelings of empathy and shared experiences to feel close to their partner. Not only do they need to "do stuff" together, but they want to talk about *why* they did it, *how* it made them both feel, *what* it all means, and *whether* they should do it again! It's easy to see how misunderstandings can occur.

So what implications does this have for *your* relationship? How can you create a successful relationship with a partner who has different emotional intimacy needs and plays by a different set of rules? Perhaps if we just stepped back and looked at it from the men's perspective for a few moments, we'd see and feel things very differently. I know, I know, it's not fair—why can't men do that so they can see how we feel? Because they are simpler creatures and we have to take the lead.

Let's look at Tony and Alison, who have been seeing each

other for a couple of months. Tony has an active social life, spending the majority of his time with friends. Alison was attracted to his outgoing nature and his ability to connect with people. She wants a committed and intimate relationship and assumes that Tony wants the same. She has interpreted Tony's social behavior as evidence that he also enjoys forging close bonds. Thus, she makes efforts to increase their level of intimacy by trying to connect with him emotionally, via romantic walks in the park, candlelit dinners for two, and "sharing sessions" every morning in bed. She has recently started to realize that Tony is resisting her efforts and actually avoiding a deep romantic connection. So Alison concludes that Tony isn't interested in a serious relationship.

But Tony's thinking is very different from Alison's conclusion. He loves making new connections but sees intimacy as something that develops slowly. Alison's efforts are considered too pushy and demanding. How could she expect to know so much about his inner workings when they are just at the "getting to know you" stage of their relationship? Ironically, the relationship will flounder, not because they don't want the same things, but because they want them at different paces and expect them to flourish in different ways. Trying to force or manufacture intimacy will usually push your partner away, not bring him closer.

HOW TO "CLOSE THE DEAL"
ON A RELATIONSHIP

Being emotionally unavailable is in essence when someone lacks what we call "emotional intelligence"—the ability to recognize how you and others feel and to use the information to create relationships. While all humans share the same basic emotional needs, they differ in the degree to which they can have those needs met or meet them for others. Some people may actually avoid making connections or expressing feelings of intimacy. For them, emotions, in all their manifestations, become a source of threat, and the possibility of experiencing, showing, talking about, or eliciting emotions in others induces a sense of vulnerability.

Obviously, lacking emotional intelligence and being emotionally unavailable is counterproductive to gaining intimacy in a relationship. Well, then, how do you go about gaining emotional intelligence? Glad you asked! There are certain abilities you need to adopt in order to display effective emotional intelligence:

1. **Self-awareness.** Observe yourself and recognize what you're feeling. *The reason I made that defensive joke about no man being reliable is because I am still working through the letdown from my last relationship. It's not fair to project unresolved feelings on someone else.*

2. **Managing your emotions.** Handle feelings appropriately; realize what is behind a feeling; find ways to deal with fears and anxieties, anger and sadness. A great way to do this is

to give an alternative explanation to the worst-case scenario that is playing in your mind. *He hasn't called, but this doesn't mean he wants to break up. I'm not going to get anxious. He's probably just busy doing something else. And so am I.*

3. Motivating yourself. Instead of dwelling on situations you cannot predict or control, channel your emotions toward positive endeavors. *I really want to know if Sam is going to call me for another date. I know he's away on business for a couple of days so I don't need to know right this minute. Instead of staring at the phone all day I'm going to keep living my life.*

4. Empathy. Be sensitive to others' feelings and concerns and appreciate the differences in the way they handle things. *Dan seems really down and moody. He said he wasn't up to going out. I guess he's tired and had a busy day at work. How could he know I'm dying to tell him about my promotion? I'll let him unwind for a while.*

5. Handling relationships. Manage other people's emotions and have good social skills. *I know he's mad with his brother for forgetting his mom's birthday, and he always gets so worked up when they have a disagreement. I'm not going to let his anger affect me. Instead I'll listen sympathetically and suggest we have everyone to dinner for a birthday celebration. That way I hope he can begin to focus on the solution rather than ranting about the problem.*

People who have not fully developed these skills may find it difficult to recognize and embrace these emotions in themselves and in others. Instead, they will probably disengage from emotional attachment to someone in a variety of ways, perhaps using humor or preoccupation as avoidance tactics. In turn, they will be perceived by their partner as emotionally unavailable, avoidant, or immature. This will obviously create a massive hurdle for the development of a romantic relationship, where intimacy, closeness, and trust are vital. Since emotional intimacy develops at different paces for everyone, don't get frustrated by your partner's apparent inability to connect as quickly as you do. The less you push, the more likely it will happen.

Remember, becoming a couple is not about pinning each other down. It's about having the tools to keep developing your emotional connection with each other. Since intimacy often means something very different for men and women, it is only when we are able to acknowledge that these differences exist that we will be able to secure the relationship we deserve. At times, it might seem almost like an impossible task for the two sexes to *ever* connect and share a bond. Yet the more you truly *listen* to your partner and actively work to meet both his and your emotional intimacy needs, the more you will find that entering coupledom is not as difficult as you once thought. You will then be free to focus your attention on all the things that go into being a couple and help your new relationship thrive.

TIPS TO REMEMBER

- Men and women have different approaches. Don't expect his needs to be the same as yours.
- Be open and honest with each other.
- The pace at which he wants to take things will probably be slower than yours. Don't rush things.
- Don't feel rejected if he doesn't want to be a couple straightaway. It doesn't mean he doesn't want to be with you.

CHAPTER 5

Let's Talk About Sex, Baby

Laura and Rob are on their sixth date, each one a roaring success. Rob is totally into Laura. She's funny, beautiful, and charming, and he's wanted to sleep with her since pretty much date number one. Laura likes Rob, too. He's exactly what she's looking for in a partner, and she wants this to turn into something serious. Rob is driving Laura home.

ROB: Should we go back to my place?

LAURA: I can't. I've got a meeting first thing in the morning.

ROB: Well, I'm closer to town . . . and I make a mean waffle breakfast.

LAURA: Tempting, but I should really sleep in my own bed. What are you doing Saturday?

ROB: Don't know yet. I'll drop you home and call
you tomorrow.

The joy of sex is well documented. It can enhance your
general happiness and emotional well-being. There's nothing better than the feeling that the person whose arms you
want to rush into wants exactly the same from you. The fact
is, when sex is good, it's really good. And most romantic
relationships will eventually end up in the bedroom. We all
know this going in. Yet sex is one of the hardest topics to
broach, especially in a new relationship, and guaranteeing
that a good sexual relationship continues to thrive requires
the efforts of both partners.

We all have our own ideas about when it should happen,
how it should go, and why it is important to us. Unfortunately, we rarely convey our concerns and thoughts to our
partner, who is left to fend for himself and look at the situation from his own skewed point of view.

The Rob and Laura situation is a prime example of two
people not communicating. Rob wants to have sex with
Laura. He is ready and thinks she should be also. They have a
great time together and he clearly wants the relationship to
grow. Despite being just as interested in having sex as Rob is,
Laura's holding back until she is certain he is serious about
her. Rob is becoming frustrated by her resistance because
he really *does* like her and can't figure out what the problem
is. Since their attitudes toward sex and its timing are so different, neither can quite get their head around the other's
preferred sexual schedule. Unfortunately, Rob bases much

of his self-confidence on his sexual ability and thus feels that Laura's reluctance to sleep with him is a snub. Laura believes that it will scare Rob off if she appears too "easy." But since Laura is not making it clear that despite her feelings she needs more time and Rob is internalizing his feelings of rejection, the relationship is in serious trouble. How is this possible, when Rob and Laura have breezed through every other obstacle their new relationship has thrown at them? Because, when sex gets introduced into a relationship, it can throw everything off course.

Why? Simply put, sex is a really important part of any relationship, and getting it right can do wonders for your success as a couple. A really good, intimate sexual bond can help overcome many general problems, just as little or no sex between an otherwise loving couple can damage the relationship. Good sex comes from good communication—being able to talk about your sexual likes and dislikes to your partner.

If sex is an important component of any romantic relationship and both men and women value it, then what is the problem? Well, as usual when discussing the genders, they view the issue completely differently.

It's not just that men and women seek sex in different ways or talk about sex differently or approach sex differently. Their attitudes to sex are totally different and they *experience* sex differently. Women want to experience a certain emotional closeness before sex, while men view sex as a route to this closeness. Women regard it as both an accompaniment to a strong relationship and a method of securing that relationship in the first place.

Men in general seem to hold more permissive attitudes toward sex. They want more sexual partners and a variety of sexual sensations. For a man, having sex may represent being loved and desired. It's a physical act that can lead to an emotional bond but they often seek sex just for the sake of sex. For women, the emotional bond is tied into the physical act and they have a more difficult time divorcing the two.

Why is it so different for him? Take a look at the following scenario:

Neil and Paula met at a party. They really hit it off, and at the end of the night they ended up at Neil's place. The following morning, Paula wakes up in Neil's arms.

> NEIL: I had a great time last night. How about you grab a hot shower, I'll brew some coffee, and then I can drive you home.
>
> PAULA: Okay. I mean, unless you want to go out to breakfast, maybe catch a matinee.
>
> NEIL: That sounds great, but I can't. Not today.
>
> PAULA: I understand. Maybe tomorrow?
>
> NEIL: I'll call you.
>
> PAULA: Sure.

You may recognize this as the legendary one night stand. Women everywhere reading this will think that Neil is just another jerk, taking advantage of a poor girl looking for a relationship. But he simply sees the situation very differently.

By definition, one night stands involve maximum excitement and minimum commitment. And unsurprisingly, men are far more interested in them than women. This is because they're far better at separating sex and emotion than women are. So after a brief postnightclub experience, while the man is likely to scratch a notch in his bedpost and move on without a second thought, the woman may well be left wondering what their encounter meant or where it will go from here. Men are likely to have a more simplistic view of sex. After all, their inclinations are far more basic than a woman's. Where a man might see a good-looking girl and instantly feel lust, the average woman will see a model-type man and think *Yeah, he's hot. So what?* These thought processes are shaped by both our physical make-up and the way men and women are taught to approach sex.

PHYSICAL DIFFERENCES

Men and women are built entirely differently. These differences affect what we actually experience physically, what stimulates us, and what we find enjoyable during sex. And even when we reach fulfillment, we experience completely different orgasms.

Mother Nature is extremely instrumental in determining our part in physical relationships. Sex hormones take center stage in the determination of sex-related behavior. They determine our sexual drive, sexual arousal, and orgasms.

Both men and women want sex as much as the other, but usually at different times and for different reasons. Men want sex at pretty regular intervals in a sort of pulsing pattern of desire. This is largely due to that infamous male hormone, testosterone. It's what makes men, well, men. It gives them their hairiness, deep voices, and sexual desire.

In women, the sex hormones are estradiol and progesterone. But the female sex drive is less predictable, occurring at sporadic intervals and dependent on different influences. In many women, there is a time of increased sexual interest when they ovulate. Everything from the way a woman walks to the odor she emits is at least to some extent regulated by these hormonal cycles.

Sexual arousal involves all five senses; however, touch is the most important for both men and women, closely followed by visual stimulation. When we are sexually attracted to someone, seeing them is foreplay, but touching will literally get the juices flowing. Ultimately, our sexual responses have developed in order to give us the best chance of fulfilling the ultimate evolutionary goal, reproduction and the continuation of the species.

In men, orgasm involves ejaculation followed by extreme pleasure. Most men are able to achieve a climax within three minutes of penetrative sex. This means that for most men, the challenge is delaying orgasm for as long as possible.

For women, however, although orgasm is important, she will probably care more about the emotional responses she gets from her partner, like seeing him express his pleasure and making her feel loved and desired. An increased bond with her partner will often heighten a woman's enjoyment of sex. Orgasm simply isn't the end all and be all for her. Bonding, emotional intimacy, and cuddling are often more important.

Because of these differences, our interpretation of what we

say to each other in sexual situations is completely different. We basically hear what we want to and assume that the other person feels and thinks in exactly the same way we do.

Lisa and Louis have been seeing each other for a few weeks. They've mastered the art of great dating, they've laughed in the face of the awkward "boyfriend-girlfriend" conversation, and they've sailed through that first bout of meeting the friends. In fact, they're feeling pretty pleased with themselves. The one area they are yet to reign supreme is in the bedroom. After some careful deliberation during which Lisa says, "I don't know if I'm ready just yet," meaning "I don't want you to stop liking me if I sleep with you" and interpreted, incorrectly, by Louis as "I'm not sure if I am sexually attracted to you," they finally get down to it.

And that's where the problems begin. Louis is nervous. He really likes Lisa, and he doesn't want to mess everything up by being the world's worst lover. In fact, he thinks, better to go straight for the kill and get it over with rather than take time over everything so that she has even more opportunity to realize that his legs (but thankfully nothing else) have turned to jelly and his palms are clammy with nervous sweat. Lisa interprets this as *I can't really be bothered with pleasing you; this is just sex to me.* Lisa is well aware of what would make the experience more pleasurable for her, but she is too nervous to convey this to her increasingly orgasm-focused partner. Plus, she assumes from his actions that he's not that interested in what she wants anyway.

Louis, thinking she is experiencing the same pleasures he is, powers on and consequently falls asleep, satisfied that he and Lisa have gotten the first time out of the way and confident things will improve. Lisa lies awake for hours wondering why he didn't care enough to consider her, then gets up and leaves, feeling used, sad, and determined to never call Louis again. Louis awakens to an empty apartment and a finished relationship, unable to comprehend what went wrong and blaming himself for all the wrong reasons.

The different significance men and women attach to sex has muddled the experience. Louis separated the sex and the relationship, assuming his bond with Lisa remains, even if the sex is something they need to work on. Lisa cannot separate the two and assumes that the unsuccessful sexual experience is indicative of Louis's feelings and evidence that the relationship is doomed to fail. Breakdown in communication at this crucial time has destroyed a potentially wonderful budding romance.

WHY WE APPROACH SEX DIFFERENTLY

Our sexuality is an integral part of our personalities. It's shaped by our physiology, body image, our social circle, and our upbringing. Aspects such as what should arouse us and what constitutes sexual behavior are learned. They are a product of the environment we live in and the lessons we learn. To understand how and why women and men approach sex differently, we need to look at this combination of biology and environment.

Men and women learn a great deal about relationships in childhood and adolescence. It is in our childhood home that we begin to learn what it means to be a boy or a girl, how adult relationships work, and how our gender determines where we fit into all of this. In fact, parents influence sexual beliefs, opinions, and attitudes more than peers, school, or the media.

For example, people whose parents conveyed unhealthy messages about sex (i.e., the belief that sex is a sin or dirty) are most likely to feel guilty about even talking about sex. Young men who grow up in a family where the father was sensitive and caring to the mother's needs and wishes, sexually and nonsexually, are more likely to go on to have similarly happy, healthy sexual relationships with women.

The values and beliefs developed in the teenage years about the opposite sex often change very little in adulthood. As a result, people enter sexual relationships with some real misconceptions about sexuality and the role of sex in a relationship. Despite moving past their posturing adolescence, many grown men view sex as an act and fear the emotional ties that stem from the act. They may shut down their feelings, fearing that those feelings make them less of a man. And, undoubtedly fooled by a few fumbling first encounters, women believe that the only part of intimacy that matters to men is the sexual intercourse. Some couples never really get beyond these misconceptions.

Society also tends to dictate that women will be more sexually naive and men will be more sexually direct and assertive. Men are expected to communicate their sexual needs and desires far more freely. Any deviations from these norms have different consequences for men and women. For example, men who aren't sexually aggressive or seem effeminate will often be mocked. For women, criticism is likely to take a different form. A women who has a "mascu-line" approach to sex, is open to the idea of casual sex, or has multiple partners puts herself in the firing line for labels such as "easy" or "slut."

Thus, men are allowed far greater sexual freedom when it comes to quantity. Women are far more focused on the qual-ity side of things, associating physical intimacy with emo-tional closeness and commitment, largely due to society's declarations that these are the qualities they should want. For women, the politics of when she should let a man have his "way," what he, and the rest of society, will think of her if she does, and how it will affect their future relationship means the move from a platonic to a sexual relationship is often fraught with worry and anxiety. It's no wonder that men approach sex with a far more relaxed attitude and the ability to see it as just a rather enjoyable little hobby, so different are the social expectations with which they have to contend.

For example, Paul and Cynthia have been on a couple of fab dates: a good movie with the right mix of gripping love story and occasional gratuitous car chase, a luscious meal in a restaurant that allowed adequate under-table opportunity for a little footsie. Now Paul is going in for the kill and has asked Cynthia over "to watch a DVD."

> PAUL: I was thinking we could stay in tonight. I'll cook for us and rent a DVD.

Paul meant *I'm ready to step this up a level physically, and that's not going to happen in another lovely restau-rant. Let's get some alone time.*

Cynthia heard *I feel comfortable enough to just "chill out" with you. This is turning into something serious.*

CYNTHIA: That sounds lovely. I'll bring the wine.

Cynthia meant *I like you, and I'm looking forward to finding out even more about you.*

Paul heard *Excellent, I'm so up for this. Can't wait for you to ravish me later, you stallion!*

Skip ahead to the date. Dinner has been eaten, the wine is flowing, and the DVD is on. Paul's mind is awash with ways to divert Cynthia (who is cuddled close to him) from the screen and get her into the bedroom. Paul has taken Cynthia's affection as a sign that she is ready for sexual intimacy, when in fact all it means is that she enjoys feeling close to him. Cue some massive misunderstanding and a rather long, lonely night for Paul, with maybe a cold shower or two thrown in.

WHERE DO WE GO FROM HERE?

As exciting and relationship enhancing as sex is, we see that it provides potential for a whole new set of communication breakdowns. The example above illustrates just one of the many ways difficulties arise. Sexual discussion is still seen as taboo, but communication really is the only way to crack these misunderstandings. Since we approach sexual encounters with our own gender-based set of anxieties, we focus on the wrong things. So while you are panicking about whether the missionary position molds your boobs into an odd shape, he'll be worrying about whether he's really doing the right thing down there. While he obsesses over the size of his penis, you'll be fretting over whether you should be shy and submissive or swinging from the chandelier.

Again, we tend to hear incorrectly, as a result of our own inner beliefs. When he says, "Was that OK for you? Did you enjoy it?" you might interpret that as "You could have been a bit livelier. I nearly dozed off halfway through." Like most relationship hurdles, when we hit a communication barrier, there can be a number of negative consequences.

For example, if a woman feels that her partner views sex as a waste of time unless it culminates in her having an orgasm, she may end up faking a response or avoiding physical encounters altogether, so as to not "let him down." A failure to convey your sexual needs to your partner can lead to frustration, anger, and eventually resentment and avoidance of the sexual relationship altogether. Just as sharing emotional needs is imperative to a healthy, successful relationship, expressing sexual needs is important to the longevity of a relationship.

But before we even get to the stage where we are expressing our sexual needs, we have to cut through the social pressures and past experiences that color our expectations about sex. Even before a couple makes it to the bedroom, each of them has been exposed to a lifetime of social pressure and most probably a handful of past sexual experiences. And this will affect all aspects of how they view sex: what they expect from sex, what they enjoy or indeed feel comfortable with, and practical issues like how long they wait before sleeping with a new partner. For instance, society suggests and rein-forces the notion that men see sex as far more important to their general well-being than women do. Likewise, women are far more worried about when to elevate attraction to physical intimacy, and the reality is that more often than not, they are chiming in with society's clock, not their own body clock. Talking about the unspoken sexual tension will alleviate it and take the pressure off each person. Avoid mind reading and assuming your partner is only after sex, is holding out on sex, or just isn't into you.

Gaining a clearer understanding of the other person's point of view will certainly untangle any misconceptions or fallacies in one's thinking. By making sure we understand what the opposite sex means by what they say and do, we can change the way we behave and consequently avoid any misunderstandings.

The closer the relationship, the happier we are to talk about our sexual needs and wants, but we want it to be a two-way process. Many men are unwilling to talk about what "feels good" for them or, more importantly, for their partner, possibly fearful of shattering the myth of the magnificent, intuitive male lover. Yet talking about sex with one's partner is the only solid way to reveal sexual desires, preferences, fears, and standards. Sharing this information promotes not only intimacy but satisfaction as well.

Let's look at the following example. Kevin and Myra are both bankers, leading busy lives. They have been dating for a month, wining, dining, and enjoying each other's company. Their first sexual encounter was good but definitely left room for a little improvement. Kevin loves the idea of Myra giving him oral sex, and Myra loves the idea of Kevin being verbally expressive while lovemaking. Instead of communicating their needs and talking about them, each partner sticks to "safe" territory, only subtly hinting at what they really want, which satisfies neither.

KEVIN: Did you enjoy that?

MYRA: Of course I did.

Kevin meant *I feel like something's not quite right here. Is it me?*

MYRA meant *I enjoy sex with you, but I just wish you were less obsessed about oral!*

KEVIN heard *It was awful!*

MYRA heard *I only care about myself.*

Instead of openly discussing their sexual encounter, they preferred to withdraw in fear of hurting each other's feelings. Their behavior was largely influenced by their own understandings. The various guesses that went on were all wrong. If they were to check them out, they would find out that their interpretations were primarily based on their own expectations, fears, and internal states. By accepting everything that was said with their own skewed interpretation, they simply set up a cycle of confusion that means two things are likely to happen. First, the chances of Myra embracing oral sex as Kevin wishes she would are fairly slim, as are the chances of Kevin communicating with Myra in the way she likes during sex. And second, this couple is destined to miss out on the strong, intimate bond that can develop through open, honest sexual communication.

Maybe a woman will assume her new lover hates oral sex because he never initiates it. Each time they get intimate and he doesn't go down on her, she interprets this as further confirmation of her suspicions. Meanwhile, maybe her partner has developed the theory that it's *she* who hates the idea because she never suggests it, and he's scared of attempting something he thinks she doesn't like. Confusing stuff. The only way to get around this is for the individuals to challenge these assumptions through verbal or nonverbal communication.

Great lovers become great because they are willing to communicate comfortably with their partner. But raising the subject can be tricky. Sex is fun, exciting, and arousing. But it can also be a particularly embarrassing business, especially when it comes to writing your sexual wish list for your partner or putting him straight on that weird toe-sucking thing he thinks you love but actually makes your skin crawl.

All this sounds complicated and messy. But there are simple ways to initiate some productive sexual discussion with your partner.

• **Sit comfortably with your partner.** Immediately after sex is not the ideal time, as everything said will sound heightened and can be easily misinterpreted. A conversation over a glass of wine will do wonders to relax the mood.

• **Raise your thoughts.** Frame your words in a positive light. If you have a complaint, avoid making it sound like negative criticism. Instead of "I hate how you concentrate exclusively on my nipples during foreplay," try saying, "I love how aroused my body gets during foreplay. You don't need to only stay at my nipples. Kissing my stomach gets me just as hot."

• **Be clear.** If ear nibbling is not your thing, say so.

• **Listen to what your partner tells you.** The purpose is for you both to be satisfied.

• **Don't be defensive.** If he tells you he doesn't like when you claw his back, don't take it as an insult or shoot back that your last boyfriend loved it. Each person is different and he is trying to tell you what he feels. Plus, it's very possible your last boyfriend hated it and was just too afraid to tell you.

Interestingly, the ability to communicate needs and feelings during intimate sexual activity often helps build better communication skills in nonsexual areas as well, solidifying the relationship as a whole. Once you get into the habit of being honest about your requirements in the bedroom, you'll probably find it easier to communicate other needs to your partner. Let's be honest, asking him to refrain from smoking in your car will seem like a breeze compared to telling him that you like being spanked.

Take time to challenge your cognitions. Why do you think the way you do? How realistic is your thinking? Is there any evidence to suggest it might be wrong? If you challenge this theory and act against it, what is the worst that can happen?

And be clear with your partner. Accept that he also has his own set of sexual prejudices and this will affect the way he reads your responses in the bedroom. He too will interpret you through a smokescreen of schemas, so communicate clearly and unashamedly. If you were in a business meeting and you were unsure of what your client was asking of you, you'd make sure you clarified it straightaway. If you went to the hairdressers, you'd want to make sure the stylist knew exactly what you wanted before she got gung-ho with the scissors. Exercise the same clarity of communication in your personal life, particularly when it comes to your sexual relationship. And embrace the fact that if you and your partner sometimes appear to be speaking different languages, at least this is the one area of your relationship where you can both let a little nonverbal communication do the talking.

TIPS TO REMEMBER

- Encourage your partner to talk to you about what he wants. And listen to the answer.
- Speak up. Don't fall prey to the myth that he should automatically know what you like and take the lead because he is a man.
- Be clear. If you mean no, then say no. Try to avoid mixed signals.

CHAPTER 6

Confronting Commitment Issues

Lucy and Mike are an exclusive couple. Their relationship has moved to the stage where one of them sleeps over at the other person's place at least four nights a week. They have both acknowledged that they love being able to wake up together in the mornings. They have just spent a romantic weekend at Mike's place, complete with candlelit dinners, plenty of snuggling, and the first appearance of the phrase "I love you."

LUCY: Thanks for a lovely time this weekend. You're such a fantastic cook.

MIKE: My pleasure. By the way, you left your toothbrush, perfume, and a pair of earrings on my bathroom shelf. I put them safely in a little bag for you to take home.

LUCY: Oh. Well, I could just leave them *here;* save me carting them back and forth each visit.

MIKE: Mmm, I'm a bit of a neat freak.

LUCY: Okay, I'll put them in the cabinet.

MIKE: There's not really enough room. It's probably easier to just pop them in your purse.

LUCY: There's no room . . . for a toothbrush?

MIKE: I'm a little uncomfortable with the situation.

LUCY: Thanks for a *lovely* weekend!

Lucy storms out.

What's going on here? Is Mike really such a bathroom neat freak or does Lucy leaving her possessions in his apartment makes him feel she's trying to force the relationship along too quickly? How is a left-behind toothbrush considered moving too fast, while a declaration of love is not? Because one is words, the other is action. Saying "I love you" makes everyone feel good; seeing symbols of that "I love you" strewn about the one-bedroom apartment can be a scary sight. The question is whether Mike is justified in his reaction or just the dreaded personality type—a commitment phobe!

It's a label bandied about far too freely these days, but what do you do if you find yourself trying to have a serious relationship with somebody who seems to be a commitment phobe? During the lovey-dovey stages of the relationship, the two of you enjoy each other's company, can't picture life without each other, and feel like you are on top of the world. It's hard not to fall in love during that time. But when signs indicate the relationship is heading for the long haul, any commitment phobe worth his salt will freak out.

IS HE OR ISN'T HE?

Before jumping into fixing your commitment-phobic boyfriend, you first need to determine if your partner is truly scared of commitment. You can't slap the label on him just because he doesn't want to discuss baby names on the fifth date or get a joint checking account after living together for a week. Now, if he still won't discuss baby names when your child is heading off to preschool, that's another story.

Too often when a man hesitates in a relationship, he is immediately accused of shying away. That's not fair. As we discussed, women are ready to commit much sooner. They are more in tune with their feelings and usually welcome a more stable relationship. But that doesn't mean you should sit idly by while your boyfriend (your word, not his, since he doesn't believe in the whole "boyfriend/girlfriend" thing) leads you on. You need to know where this relationship is going, and a man who is capable of committing will take your concerns seriously. He may not respond every time you want reassurance, but he will be able to participate in discussions about your joint future.

How will you know if your partner is displaying commitment-phobic tendencies? It's all about listening and picking up clues. If he never wants to discuss where the relationship is heading, skirts any topic having to do with long-term plans, or pushes away efforts to have an emotional connection, you may be with a commitment phobe. How you handle it is important. If you push, you may lose him altogether, but you do need to get answers, if only to protect your own heart.

Let's go back to the opening scenario. Lucy and Mike seem to be getting along great. Yet when Mike reacts strongly to a toothbrush, Lucy reacts back and storms out of the apartment, and quite possibly the relationship. It left her, and us, wondering what's going on. Instead of leaving and spending the rest of the week confused, Lucy should talk to Mike and get her answers.

MIKE: I'm a little uncomfortable with the situation.

LUCY: Okay. I just thought we were moving in the right direction.

MIKE: We are. It's going to sound silly, but having your stuff here is a big step for me. My last girlfriend did that and suddenly we were living together and I wasn't ready. I don't want that to happen with us. I want to take it a little slower.

LUCY: But we did the "I love you" thing.

MIKE: I do love you. But I know me, and I need a little more time. Don't worry. We'll get there.

WHY HE WON'T COMMIT

It may not be what Lucy wants to hear, but now she can better understand where Mike is coming from. To her, it's a toothbrush, which is logical to leave at his place. To him, it's an express train to a messy breakup, based on his previous experience. By talking about it, Lucy is able to open up the lines of communication instead of being left in the dark, and Mike is comfortable enough to express his fears.

The inability to commit can stem from many factors. Obviously, there are people out there who just don't want to settle down. They like being able to play the field, and no matter what you feel the connection is, they are not ready to be exclusive. Sure, there may be psychology at work, but it probably won't be worthwhile trying to unearth the reason behind the behavior.

More often, the fear of commitment is a fear of opening up. People who can't commit are protecting themselves from getting hurt. The tough part is they fear the very thing they crave: the love and attention a relationship would give. But don't despair. It is possible to break through his hesitancy and anxiety.

If you find your partner is afraid of commitment, be prepared for a rocky road. Attempting to grow close to someone with an active fear of opening up and getting close can be relentlessly frustrating and often very painful. Usually, the more you try to penetrate the inner layers of somebody who has a distinct fear of being exposed, the more he will close up and resist your efforts. People who have a history of experiencing difficulties in forming close emotional bonds may reflect this in the treatment of their partners. They can be cold, dismissive, or even cruel.

Building an intimate bond with a partner can trigger a person's inner fear of risk and danger. He might find it difficult to vocalize his true thoughts and beliefs for fear of stirring up some of these difficult emotions. So it seems easier simply to withdraw and stifle any feelings before he "loses control."

For people who feel this way, being asked to open up is like entering unknown and potentially dangerous territory. Their dysfunctional thinking process tells them, *I can't go there; I mustn't let that happen,* but they are not comfortable vocalizing or explaining this inner dialogue. In fact emotionally unavailable people will go out of their way to avoid saying what feels even slightly emotional. This kind of anxiety or fear of intimacy can be categorized into three distinctive viewpoints.

1. People who show their feelings are weak. Jasmine dated Frank for three months and felt their relationship was really going somewhere. They got along fantastically and had great fun on dates. But recently Frank was having some problems at work, which made him feel down. Jasmine really wanted to help, but every time she tried to talk to him he simply said, "It's fine. It's no big deal. I don't need your sympathy." This dismissal made Jasmine feel rejected, as if Frank didn't feel close enough to her to share his problems. It made her doubt the relationship.

But if Jasmine were to challenge her own viewpoint, she might realize that the problem was not that Frank didn't care enough about Jasmine, but that his family had entrenched in him the view that "real men" didn't mope around worrying. Men in his family were expected to fix their problems on their own.

This kind of belief is a common reason why men often don't talk about how they feel. They suppress their emotions because they have a fixed idea of what experiencing emotions *means*. Typical meanings include weakness or vulnerability on the man's part, and experiencing such feelings may be seen as nonmasculine and threaten the view he has of himself as a strong, self-sufficient person.

2. If I show emotion I'll be rejected. Louise had been with Colin for a month and really liked him but was getting confusing signals. Even though he always arranged the next date immediately after the previous one ended and called and e-mailed her every day, he hadn't actually said he was "into" her. In fact, when she asked him how he thought things were going she was met with an embarrassing silence. After hours of worrying, she decided to come right out and say, "I really like you. Do you feel the same?" Colin replied, "Yes, I'm so glad you told me. I was worried *you* weren't into me!"

Like Colin, some men hold a fixed belief, usually based on a previous bad experience from childhood or former relationship, that showing emotion will result in them getting hurt. They think of themselves as inadequate or even unlovable. It took Louise acting bold and admitting her feelings before Colin could allow himself to say he liked Louise—safe in the knowledge that he wouldn't be rejected.

3. I don't know how I really feel. It was five months in and Jack and Janie were having a good time. They loved each other's company and always had a blast together. The only blot on the horizon was when Janie asked Jack if he loved her and he replied, "I think so, but I don't know for sure." This honest uncertainty devastated her. And here he thought he'd made a brave attempt at identifying a tricky emotion.

Many men have difficulty working out and then saying how they feel. Being unable to label feelings or understand their significance often causes confusion and uncertainty and can provoke a wide variety of reactions. A guy may feel miraculously overjoyed or as if something is missing from his life without the faintest idea of why he feels this way. He may avoid sharing his emotions, because he simply doesn't know how to put them into words.

The inability to articulate emotion often comes from the fact that someone is so focused on problem solving—i.e., on attaining particular feelings or getting rid of others—that he doesn't stop and just let himself *feel*. This is more often a male problem, as men tend to be problem solvers by nature. They want a logical explanation for everything—including love!

THE PARENT TRAP

As grown-ups, we enter intimate relationships with a ready-made, well-established set of beliefs. Many of these beliefs develop from experiences in early family life and continue to manifest themselves in similar ways throughout our adult lives. For instance, in any relationship we tend to seek close proximity and love when we're experiencing distress. A four-year-old who fell over and wants a hug and a bandage from Mommy mirrors the actions of twenty-four-year-old who flunked her first job interview and just wants a cup of hot chocolate and a hug from her boyfriend. The basic care needs are remarkably similar.

People's beliefs not only affect how they think about relationships and behave, but they also influence how they respond emotionally within intimate relationships. Since these beliefs are learned, our early life can stunt adult emotional growth and plague our intimate relationships, to varying degrees. There are certain syndromes people suffer from as a result of previous experiences:

1. **"Product of the past" syndrome.** Lena is a thirty-five-year-old woman who suffered a sexually abusive childhood. She finds it very difficult to trust others and she has never had a long-term relationship with a man. Until she went to college she avoided dating. In the first two years away from home, she started going out with friends and doing drugs. Only then was she able to be intimate with men. The experience of the sexual abuse by her stepfather damaged her trust in others and her capacity for intimacy with men. She becomes angry and anxious with any man who seems to approach her romantically. She finds it hard to challenge the belief that "men are only out for sex" when one asks her out on a date or pays her a compliment. Lena cannot trust and build bonds with men, because her early childhood relationships didn't show her

how to do this successfully. She has never been in an environment built on strong interpersonal attachments, so she is unsure of how to build and maintain them. Conversely, a person with secure experience of bonding with others is likely to have positive beliefs about herself and others and therefore will approach relationships expecting closeness and intimacy. Lena's basic belief is *Men can't be trusted.*

2. **"Never good enough" syndrome.** Aaron is a thirty-two-year-old Wall Street banker. He has been through a series of relationships but none have lasted long. Every time he starts dating he gets carried away with the excitement that she is "the one." But, despite this initial attraction, his relationships always end up in disappointment. The chemistry disappears early on and his partners always end up boring him. He feels intensely alone and shows a tendency to be demanding in his romantic relationships. Nothing a new partner has to offer is ever good enough for him because he lets little things become huge disappointments.

Perhaps in his past, he was let down by a father who promised things and didn't deliver. And he carried this "hoping for the best, expecting the worst" attitude into his early relationships, where he was inevitably let down. Thus, Aaron is always waiting for the other shoe to drop and assumes his partner will fail him. Anything she does that does not meet his expectations is distorted and unforgivable. Aaron finds it hard to challenge his basic belief: *The women I meet don't understand me and can never fulfill my needs.*

3. "Rabbit in the headlights" syndrome. Henry, a twenty-six-year-old teacher, grew up in a volatile household where he learned that the easiest way to keep the peace was by constantly trying to please his parents while ignoring his own needs. A very good looking guy with a big circle of friends, he is quite popular with women, as he seems to be genuinely sensitive. However, he feels trapped in all his romantic relationships. His easygoing and eager-to-please nature causes him to always strive to meet the needs of his partner. In doing this though, he ends up not satisfying on his own needs. Always trying to satisfy his partner to his own detriment wears on Henry until he finds it hard to challenge his automatic belief that when his date makes a suggestion, she intends to control him or infringe on the lifestyle he loves so much.

So, when Henry continues to believe that his partner wants to change him and make demands on him, initially he will bend over backward to meet her every need, regardless of whether this is necessary or not. Eventually, Henry will start to resent these little unsolicited sacrifices and the relationship will fail. This will only serve to reinforce Henry's beliefs that women want too much from him. Much of this thought process occurs without his partner having any idea what's going on. His basic belief is *A relationship is too much work and will rob me of my independence.*

4. "The closed book" syndrome. Myra is an attractive twenty-nine-year-old lawyer. She wants to be with someone but always finds that her relationships end in disaster. She is open to falling in love but is unable to get really close to someone.

Her partners usually describe her as distant. Her parents were never really affectionate and she learned to keep her emotions bottled up. She can't let go of the belief that her partner will find emotional expression inappropriate. Her basic belief is *Everything has to be kept inside. If I show emotion, I will lose control.*

In the above examples, set beliefs influence aspects of behavior in relationships. And often, the behavior leads to outcomes that only strengthen the basic beliefs. It's a vicious cycle that is hard to escape and becomes a self-fulfilling prophecy.

It's clear that being around healthy, happy partnerships not only helps us to build good relationships, but also helps us cope when things go wrong or when we are feeling down. Being able to show vulnerability or inner pain to your partner is hugely important within a relationship.

HOW TO HELP A COMMITMENT PHOBE COMMIT

"Closeness" and "intimacy" are important buzzwords within a relationship. As with any relationship, not feeling like our emotional requirements are being met can produce a variety of responses ranging from frustration to despair. And a fear of commitment may be one of the first big hurdles your relationship faces, as it wreaks havoc with the process of cementing a new partnership.

It's vital that each partner is clear about what kind of emotional bond he or she expects or requires within a relationship. Sharing how you feel is an integral part of emotional communication, but it's one that commitment phobes find tough, so approach it slowly and progressively. Asking questions about your partner's feelings is only the first step. You need to make sure you reveal your own emotions as well so you can create a positive two-way interaction, rather than a one-way interrogation!

One way to do this is ask empathetic questions, which show that you understand how the other person is feeling. It allows you to get a deeper understanding of your partner's emotions. Instead of asking, "Why are you being such a moody idiot today?" say, "You seem a little distant. Talk to me about how you're feeling." The approach encourages a reluctant person to respond more and produces more open results.

Giving a positive response when your partner opens up to you encourages him to open up more in the future. If you listen and offer understanding rather than overreact when your partner shares something like "Sometimes I worry about getting close to you, because I'm scared you might hurt me or leave me," you then have an open avenue to discuss these fears and grow together as a couple. The more the lines of communication open, the more likely your partner will continue to offer these kinds of insights in the future.

Don't forget, this is about sharing. If you want to persuade your partner to confide in you, then make sure you confide in him, too, instead of turning to your girlfriends for emotional support. Here are some tips to help both you and your partner uncover commitment issues:

• **Understand your own feelings.** Emotions alert us about what needs are not being met. For example, when we feel lonely or when we feel rejected, it is our need for acceptance that is being neglected. Learn how to interpret and respond to your emotions.

• **Listen and talk in equal measure.** Talking about your feelings will help you express your emotional needs and give you the best chance of fulfilling them, but effective listening will give you insight into his problems and may also allow you to see your own needs in a different light.

• **Be aware that he might not communicate as easily as you.** Using emotional language and talking about feelings is generally easier for women. Be patient if he is not saying exactly what you expect him to say.

• **Feel good about saying how you feel.** If you feel confident expressing emotions, it's likely to encourage sharing and help you bond on a deeper level.

• **Own your emotions.** It's much easier for a man to listen and respond effectively to "I know you are really busy at work but sometimes I feel like I'm not that important when you forget to call me back" rather than "By never returning my calls when you're at work, it's clear that you don't care about me." It's softer and sounds less like an accusation.

The more you can share how you're really feeling with each other, the less the potential for awkward conversations and misunderstandings. Instead of stumbling around a conversation unsure why your partner is reacting a certain way, you will be able to confront situations head-on.

Let's take a look at Christian and Jenny. Christian is terrified that letting his guard down to a woman will give her license to lock him up and control his life. Feelings freak him out and cause him to shrink from emotional intimacy. He has just begun a new relationship with Jenny. They've been dating for two months and so far it's going well. Jenny seems laid back and cool about things, and Christian has so far managed to stifle any claustrophobic feelings. One day they happen to watch a documentary about social workers who find families for war orphans. Jenny is obviously moved, and an awkward silence descends.

> CHRISTIAN: Are you OK? (*Oh, no. What's going on here? I never know what to do when a girl cries.*)

> JENNY: Sure, I just find this a little hard to watch. My parents both died by the time I was twenty and it hit a nerve.

Silence.

Christian thinks *What's this documentary got to do with your life? I know that must have been hard for you, but this is totally unrelated. I don't know how to deal with your emotions and it makes me feel awkward and trapped.*

> JENNY: It's a long story and we don't need to talk about it now if you don't want to.

Silence.

> JENNY: (*I'm opening up to you here. You could be a tad more comforting. This is a big deal to me.*) I'm

sorry to burden you with this. (*I shouldn't have to apologize for my emotions.*)

CHRISTIAN: That's fine, don't worry about it. (*Good, now we can go back to being normal. That was uncomfortable.*)

Christian and Jenny don't understand each other's emotional viewpoints. He can't commit to her because he can't cope with her feelings, much less comprehend what she needs. For him, any trip down an emotional road spells doom, and he is determined to avoid that. Consequently, Christian doesn't recognize that Jenny wants to share with him to allow them to become closer, and his confused reaction reflects that. Jenny takes offense at his unwillingness to let her open up because she doesn't understand his confusion. Had either of the pair understood how their basic differences affected their viewpoints and consequently their reactions, they would be far closer to finding a common emotional language.

They may be in separate places, but Jenny and Christian can bridge the gap. Jenny can't assume that Christian is in the same place as she is. But she can tell him that she would love to be able to open up to him and let him in emotionally. He may not be comfortable about it at that very moment, but emotions are now on the table. Instead of unburdening herself emotionally all at once, Jenny can take baby steps, letting him in a little at a time. The less overwhelming and threatening the whole process seems, the more likely Christian will be to reciprocate. As he gets his feet wet and sees that sharing feelings isn't life or death, he'll eventually be ready to go into the water, and the relationship will grow naturally.

Commitment to an emotionally intimate relationship can be tricky. Go slowly, go surely, and don't expect anything of your partner that you aren't comfortable with yourself. If you want him to open up about past relationships, then try sharing with him first. If you don't think he's being honest about his feelings after a big fight, then talk to him about yours, without the blame, the screaming, and the swearing. Emotional bonding is a two-way street, and once you get it right, your relationship will be ready to progress to the next level.

TIPS TO REMEMBER

- Just because men take things much more slowly than women, it doesn't necessarily mean he's a commitment phobe. Make sure *you're* not rushing things.
- Don't interpret withdrawal as rejection. Give your partner space to deal with emotions in a way that he feels comfortable with.
- Don't try to trap him. He'll run.
- If you're asking him to share his innermost feeling, be willing to show yours first.

Meeting the In-Laws

Helen and Andrew have dated seriously for a year. Andrew is anxious for Helen to meet his parents, as he is very close to them. Helen, aware of how important this meeting is to him, is determined to make a good impression.

> HELEN: It's so great to finally meet you. I brought a homemade chocolate cake for you.

> ANDREW'S MOM: How sweet. I'll save it for later. I've set out some snacks since you're not staying for a proper meal.

> ANDREW: I'm sorry we can't stay for dinner. Helen's got some work to do this evening. Her boss is really demanding.

> ANDREW'S MOM: Goodness, sounds very high

powered. I'm just so glad *I* was never a career girl. Well, I never needed to be with your father doing so well . . .

HELEN: It's not a problem, I can delay the report until tomorrow if you'd prefer.

ANDREW'S MOM: No, no dear, you must do what you have to do.

This first meeting with Andrew's mom is likely to have made Helen want to lock herself in the bathroom for the rest of the night. Meeting future in-laws is one of the most nerve-racking experiences any new couple goes through. Much as we may like to think that our other half's life began the day we met them, it just isn't true. No, before us there was his mother washing his socks, ironing his underwear, and cultivating that rather irritating tendency he has to leave both on the living room floor.

The reality is that whenever a new relationship begins, each partner will bring a host of family (and family dynamics) into the equation. Just as we all bring emotional history and relationship-related preconceptions with us when we start up with a new partner, we also bring a bevy of key characters whose opinions are important to us, and who, to some extent, affect our beliefs and behavior. This is a natural progression to the relationship as we integrate a new person into the wider parts of our lives. And as always, being a man or a woman affects the way we perceive and address the challenges this presents.

There are a number of issues that you and your partner will face before you even begin making formal introductions. The first problem is timing. It's easy to avoid putting a name to your relationship when it's just the two of you, existing in your own little world with no need for definitions. But the minute you choose to introduce your new partner to the other important people in your life, they suddenly require a title. You can't really leave "This is Matt, my . . ." as an open-ended statement. Introducing your partner to your mom is often interpreted as a less direct way of saying "I think you're going to feature heavily in my future, therefore I think it is important that you meet those who are also an important part of my life." And for a lot of people, that's a little bit scary.

Then there are the "What if they hate each other?" fears. Obviously your family is important to you. Realistically, you want both your family and your new partner in your life for ever and ever, and more than that, you want them both to actually grow fond of each other. But the problem is that when people care about us, they justifiably have very high expectations for the way our lives play out. Now your boyfriend may not be the ax-wielding monster your mother seems to think he is, but more often than not, her warped view of him won't be related to who he really is. It will be tied in with who he isn't. Letting new members into a group can be stressful, and when we are stressed it is easier to develop an unrealistically clear-cut view of a situation, where people are either "victims" or "villains." Your mother probably always had a very precise view of the man she envisioned you marrying. When you bring home your Prince Charming and he doesn't quite match up with her predictions or wishes, it can be a bitter pill to swallow.

Then of course there are the politics. Trying to feel involved and at home when you don't know family history, like where Grandpa always sits or what Aunt Sue said to Cousin Laura to make her cry at her sister's anniversary party, can really make you feel like an outsider. Equally, if you suddenly find yourself getting dragged into ongoing family arguments, you'll probably wish you were more of an outsider and weren't suddenly expected to take a stand and have a view on every family flashpoint.

Such challenges can affect the life of the couple profoundly. The new partner can feel caught up in family dynamics. You need to develop your "couple style," while still building and maintaining relations with each other's families and navigating your way through this minefield, by finding a common language.

COUPLE STYLE

Developing a couple style is important when facing outside stresses. Basically, couple style is the way in which the two of you interact within your relationship and the way you take on outside conflict and threats to your relationship. When meeting the in-laws, you need to have a united front and be clear with each other how you want to handle attacks, perceived or blatant, and difficulties that arise. An example of a strong couple style is your partner warning you that his mother can be critical but asking you not to respond in kind.

It is then up to him to nip his mother's comments in the bud while you stay civil. Thus you don't feel unprotected from his mother's sharp tongue and he doesn't worry about a full-scale war. Your couple style will help the two of you stand as a united front without added drama.

PATTERNS OF FAMILY INTERACTION

The structure of a family and the traditions and routines it holds dear will be hugely influential in the way the family accepts new members. If your boyfriend comes from a very close family, where everyone is used to having a say, or his mother is a bit controlling, they may find it hard to accept that an outsider has some claim on their son or brother. This kind of possessiveness means that it is extremely difficult, but absolutely essential, for the couple to maintain their boundaries and establish which parts of their relationship they want to share with the family and which parts are kept strictly between themselves, like him not discussing your arguments with his mother or the two of you agreeing to reserve Saturdays as a strict "no family" day.

For at least eighteen years, if not more, we are hugely dependent on our parents and the family we grow up in. And people like to feel needed. It can be a big deal for your family if they feel you are distancing yourself from them or ceasing to need their love and care. Some parents worry that their adult children might "divorce" them emotionally and become too distant. This is a natural fear, and entirely un-derstandable, if it's acknowledged and addressed. However, some parents will completely refuse to accept that their children have grown up and are ready to live independently of them. They might try to keep the status quo and not acknowledge their son's or daughter's partner as being important in their lives.

Let's look at Ryan and Meredith. They are spending another afternoon with his parents. Meredith spends the time swiftly sidestepping swipe after swipe about her hair, her job, and her family from his mother, and she slowly realizes she will never be anything other than the cheap hussy who robbed Ryan from his mother's nest. As Meredith desperately attempts to use her eyebrows to silently communicate "If you don't jump in here and defend me, we're leaving" to Ryan, he just shrugs with a dopey grin and goes back to discussing the NBA playoffs with his father. Later on they discuss the day's events.

> MEREDITH: You and your dad were having fun today, weren't you?

Meredith meant *That sucked for me.*

> RYAN: Yeah, it's great to see him. And Mom too.

> MEREDITH: Hmmm, sure.

Ryan heard *Not really.*

> RYAN: What's that supposed to mean?

> MEREDITH: Well, you could have involved me a little more, or at least stuck up for me when your mother decided to launch into her character assassination.

Ryan heard *I hate your mother.*

RYAN: (*How ungrateful! My mother invites her into her home and all Meredith can do is be rude.*) Well, perhaps you should make a little more effort. My mom is harmless. My last girlfriend and Mom were practically joined at the hip.

Meredith heard *My last girlfriend is better than you.*

The conversation continues, gradually resulting in a climactic screaming match. The expectations, pressures, and individual gender interpretations of the situation result in a big fat mess. As a woman, Meredith overanalyzes the undertones of her interaction with Ryan's mom and is always focused on how their relationship is defined. As a man, Ryan fails to see the emotional intricacies and subtext of the relationship between the two women in his life and oversimplifies the problem, hurting Meredith's feelings in the process. Nobody benefits when these destructive and awkward scenarios develop. In fact, relationship dynamics like this can drive a wedge between the partner and the family and rule out any genuine intimacy or affection. It also makes it ten times harder for the person caught in the middle, who wants desperately for the two sides to get along. Consequently, the task each partner faces is maintaining both relationships without losing either.

HOW TO DEAL WITH PARENTS

Tim is an only child who feels that he can never meet his parents' expectations. He's never been particularly close to them and has avoided them more and more as he has gone through life, seeing them only on birthdays and at Christmas. Megan comes from a large, close family where whoever shouts the loudest is the one heard, and family gatherings resemble a prison riot, only with less violence and more shrieking. Megan loves the madness of an evening with her family and tries to see them at least once a week. Now, over the years, Tim has cultivated a negative image of himself: *I am no good in social situations, people don't like me, and I am difficult to get along with.* When he meets Megan's family, his instinct is to remain detached and quiet, a tactic that works perfectly with his own family. Of course, this means that he never really bonds with Megan's rowdy relatives, and they find this hard to understand. In addition, Tim feels even more isolated and uses his strained relationship with his girlfriend's family to further confirm his negative beliefs about himself. Tim's history of family relationships and his feelings about them are massively influential in the way he connects, or rather fails to connect, with Megan's family. And so a self-fulfilling prophecy continues.

Most people worry about their interactions with their partner's parents, largely because they tap into fears about acceptance and validation from others. These are common worries and they are not always irrational or inaccurate. Sometimes relationships with your partner's parents can be tense. The situation *is* an awkward one. Just because you hit it off with your boyfriend after two glasses of a wine and a Caesar salad doesn't mean you and his mother will necessarily share the same instant bond. Realistically, you are trying to force a relationship, and that will always feel a little awkward in the beginning. But the last thing you should do is ruminate for hours about what this means and analyze exactly what it is about your behavior, background, or appearance that is preventing you from becoming best friends with his older sister. This won't alleviate the tension, and it won't make you feel any better. If anything, it will simply make you feel more awkward. Clearly gender plays a part here, as we know that women are more prone to this exhaustive and counterproductive analysis than men.

For example, let's look at David and Sophie. They've been going out for three months, and over the course of a week both arrange to meet the other's parents. Here's how the meeting goes between Sophie and David's mom:

> DAVID'S MOM: So lovely to meet you. Can I get you a drink?
>
> SOPHIE: (*Will she think badly of me if I say yes?*) Just a small glass of wine, thanks.
>
> DAVID'S MOM: Medium or dry, dear?
>
> SOPHIE: (*Oh god, she's testing my wine knowledge. She obviously doesn't think I'm classy enough for her son.*)

Even the simplest of questions evokes a bout of overanalysis and mild panic, as Sophie tries to second-guess the meaning behind every sentence. Now we go to the first meeting between David and Sophie's dad:

> SOPHIE'S DAD: Can I get you a beer?

David heard *Can I get you a beer?*

DAVID: Sure.

And the differences between common male interaction and common female interaction become clear. In fact, feelings of inadequacy are commonly expressed by girlfriends in the presence of a mother-in-law, but not often by boyfriends in the presence of their in-laws. Once again, the way we feel about a situation often comes down to the beliefs we bring to it.

If your problems with his family are more serious than a little tension here and there, this doesn't necessarily mean your relationship is doomed. It might mean you won't be sharing those idyllic holidays in Tuscany with the in-laws that you had pictured, but there are ways to ensure your relationship can exist alongside your partner's relationship with his family. And although we have talked at great length about the advantages of confronting issues, an awkward family dynamic often calls for the opposite. If you are not expected to socialize with your partner's family on a regular basis, then the power of "keeping the peace" should never be underestimated. These techniques can be used to help you deal with your partner's family more effectively and maintain socially appropriate relationships (even with people you might not like):

1. **Bite your tongue.** Everybody knows the difference between you saying your mother's a pain in the backside and somebody else saying your mother's a pain in the backside.

No matter how many millions of names your partner uses to describe his family, there is little chance that he will appreciate you expressing the same sentiments. Family is a strange thing. Despite the disagreements and conflicts, there is usually a strong survival instinct that teaches us to defend our loved ones from criticism. You won't do your relationship any favors if you join in the battles. Remember, nobody really understands a family outside of the people who are actually in the family. Don't be drawn into assuming his parents are 100 percent right or 100 percent wrong. Where possible, reserve judgment and stay out of it.

2. Don't be the middleman. You probably have enough contentious issues within your own family to not want to start playing referee to his family's disagreements as well. If the problem doesn't directly involve you, don't be tempted to get involved and act as mediator, member of the jury, or head cheerleader. It simply isn't your responsibility and it will only lead to conflict down the line. One of the rules of family love is that you always forgive. You fight, you sulk, and then eventually you remember how much you care for one another and everything blows over. But since you are not a part of the family, saying "Yeah, I totally agree with your son. You are a moaning old dragon" will stay on your record far longer than it will stay on his. Let your partner deal with his family.

3. Be on the side of reconciliation. In every family dispute there are three sides to the story—his side, their side, and the truth. In conflict, there is rarely a clear-cut right or wrong. The people on both sides of any argument are likely to believe that they are absolutely right, so the chances of agreeing on this are slim. Detach yourself enough to look at the situation objectively, no matter how unreasonable you think his family is being. Supporting reconciliation is far more useful than vowing to support your partner's feelings, no matter how unjustified his family's behavior or how unhelpful they are. Equally, trying to take the family's side will never help your relationship with your partner in the long run, because he will feel that when the going gets tough, he can't rely on you to support him. Remain impartial, calm, and focused on working things out. Constructive, calm discussion will also be more effective and less damaging than fighting fire with fire and opting for conflict.

4. You are the two most important people. When you and your partner face external pressures, you must focus inward and remember why it is that you are together. If his parents or his sister or his brothers continually place stress on your relationship, try to ensure that the utmost priority in each of your minds is looking after each other. Often, placing too much emphasis on what's not working in a relationship defocuses you about what *is* working. It can also give credence to something that doesn't deserve it. Instead of getting too engaged in pettiness with his sister, you and your partner should work out ways to accept that life places pressure on relationships but you can always work through it together.

5. Take the high road. If it does involve you, always remember this: Winning the argument is futile if in the process you manage to damage relationships permanently. While it is important to stick to your beliefs and stand up for yourself, sometimes keeping the peace and keeping quiet in the knowledge that you are right can be far more powerful. If your aim is to win every battle, then you may well do so. But it won't do your personal relationships any favors.

6. Be realistic. Yes, we know that the dream is finding a partner whose family is the mirror image of your own, who has a mother who shares your dress size, taste in clothes, and cooks a mean roast, and a father who is always available for some down-home advice. In a dream world, his sister becomes as close to you as your sister and his brother asks you for dating and fashion advice. But as we all know, the dream world rarely bears much resemblance to the real world. Accept that you can't get on with everyone and that this isn't a sign that you have failed in any way. The goal should be a situation where everyone can at least get along, even if you can't become the next Brady Bunch. Accept differences and maintain appropriate relationships that keep the peace.

7. Avoid making attacks personal. "You are a selfish old hag" sounds very different from "I think your behavior is a little inconsiderate." Learn the difference between criticizing behavior and performing a character assassination. People are more open to listening if it sounds like you are making a judgment on one incident or one aspect of their behavior, as opposed to making a judgment on their personality as a whole. Consider the language you use carefully.

8. Listen. How many times have you started a sentence with "Don't take this the wrong way . . . " or "I know you'll hate this, but . . ."? Too often we figure we already know exactly what the response will be in a given situation. We stop listening and only hear our inner dialogue. And this inevitably means people are less likely to relate to us. Never underestimate the importance of actually listening to somebody rather than simply acknowledging that they are talking.

Seth and Bethany have been seeing each other for two months, and they've decided it's time to bite the bullet and meet the parents. Bethany suggests that Seth's parents come over to her apartment for dinner one night. She starts planning the million ways she will wow them with her culinary genius and charming dinner party wit. The food is ready, the aperitifs are served, and she asks Seth to give her a hand with serving. Then it happens. Mother-in-law syndrome strikes, and Seth's mom announces, "Oh dear, I'm sure you can handle it. Let him relax and enjoy his meal."

Bethany stops in her tracks and waits for Seth's response, knowing full well that this could go one of two ways. Seth might say, "Thanks, Mom, you're right" and risk the eternal wrath of his new girlfriend. Or he might, heeding the lessons of this chapter, decide that he can respect his mom *and* his relationship in one fell swoop. Consider this response: "Mom, you've always brought me up to help around the home and I'm not going to start forgetting that now! Bethany spent ages cooking a great meal. I'll go and bring it in for us." Mom is flattered and girlfriend is calmed.

Research has found that contrary to decades of jokes

about men and their troublesome mothers-in-law, women often have the worst time bonding with their partner's family—in particular their partner's mother. As women increasingly juggle families and careers, many of them find the older generation unsympathetic or unwilling to support their choices. And really, the feeling this evokes boils down to the basic premise of any interaction with people who are important to your partner: *Am I good enough?* Obviously, you love your partner, and it follows that you want the people he loves to love you, too. That applies to his mother, his father, or his very best friend. The real issue here is making relationships work and balancing the expectations you and your partner may have of what exactly that means and how you think the relationship should take shape.

When dealing with any relationship issue it is important to acknowledge and respect each other's boundaries. Just because you limit your family occasions to Christmas and birthdays doesn't mean your new partner will be used to the same routine. Our families, our friends, and the relationships we build all contribute to our own individual set of boundaries, which determine what we feel comfortable with and how we want our life to be. All through life we must assess how flexible our boundaries are, which ones we should stick to resolutely, and which ones we can compromise. This is never more the case than when negotiating the setup of a new relationship. Our friends and family are hugely influential in our lives and we are likely to have some very strong feelings about how well we should know our partner and how much time we want to spend with them.

Incorporating the same skills and rationality into building

your bond with your partner's family that you cultivate in your relationship with him is a good place to start. But the real key here is accepting that your partner's boundaries and expectations will be different from yours, which means a little negotiation is in order. Establish a routine and a structure that works for both of you. Make sure that both sets of boundaries are being respected. Where the conflict doesn't involve you, stay detached and impartial. Where the conflict does involve you, make an effort to create a situation that is at least bearable, if not beneficial, for everyone involved. If your partner is important to you, then his friends and family should also be important to you, not least because they make up a huge part of the reasons he became the person you love so much. Take the time to build bonds with them, encourage your partner to do the same with your loved ones, and establish a couple style that will laugh in the face of all those mother-in-law jokes.

TIPS TO REMEMBER

- Don't worry about whether or not his mom becomes your best friend. Rather, let the relationship progress naturally and take it one day at a time.
- Accept that in life, we can't get along with everyone. As long as the involved parties can be civil and respectful, then there shouldn't be a problem.
- No matter how close you are to your family and friends, you both have a duty to protect your relationship as a couple and nurture it.

Moving in Together

Alice and Richard have dated for two years and Richard spends every night over at her place. Some mornings he complains about not having his stuff handy and the extra commute time.

ALICE: I was thinking it seems stupid for us both to be paying mortgages, especially since we're together all the time. Why don't you rent out your place and move into mine?

RICHARD: Um, well, it's not that simple. It could take ages to find good tenants and even then it can be asking for trouble. A guy at work ended up getting his apartment trashed when he rented it out.

ALICE: But we'd have much more money for holidays and going out. And it would make things so much easier. We'd get to wake up in the same bed every morning and both be at home.

RICHARD: Let's talk about it again in six months when things are quieter at work.

This conversation is repeated many times, in many different ways, with couples all over the world. And it tends to be the same old story. The girlfriend wants to move in, while the boyfriend is reluctant to make that extra commitment. But why is it that men and women have such different attitudes when it comes to living together? It's an inevitable progression if a couple is to last, yet when a relationship hits the "moving in together" talk, there can be all sorts of problems.

Studies show that both sexes benefit emotionally from long-term relationships. Not only are people in stable relationships less likely to suffer from depression, they're also likely to report higher levels of happiness and contentment. However, while men seem to benefit more from just living with a partner, women are better off emotionally when they actually marry. Why do men and women experience things so differently?

Women certainly crave more security in a relationship, and having a ring on your finger implies more stability and permanence. Just living together doesn't feel as secure. Men, on the other hand, are happier when they are less committed. This is clearly a breeding ground for conflict, especially when a relationship hits that stage when living together becomes top of the discussion agenda.

Men and women view the idea of moving in together entirely differently. She views commitment in terms of what she will gain and sees it as cementing their love. He sees it in terms of what he will lose and thus views it as restrictive. This helps explain why many women find it so hard to get their man past the first hurdle. For men, living together feels like one step closer to marriage.

Certainly, cohabitation is a major step for any relationship, and it is becoming increasingly commonplace. You know you're pretty serious about each other. You've explored the depths of each other's personalities to unearth the good, the bad, and the unmentionable (your singing and his hygiene habits), and you're almost sure that he's the one you were dreaming of while enduring disappointing first loves and, years later, a string of demoralizing dates. It's the normal next step, right?

This just goes to show how much the traditions of love and marriage have changed in recent times. Thirty years ago, you would be picking bridal gowns in virginal white quicker than you could say "Something borrowed, something blue . . ." The accepted process looked something like this: meet, court, get engaged, get married, move in, live happily (or not) ever after. Nowadays, committing to marriage before a period of cohabitation is less and less common. There is a huge trend toward testing the waters before jumping in for good.

Back in the day, your mother's mother would have needed to find a well-to-do man to marry her so that she ceased to be a financial burden on her father. Relationships were often inseparable from economics, and money played as big a part in marital matches as love did. But with equality has come the reality that now, most women fly the nest and become financially independent long before they even think about marriage. Our improved education, career prospects, and financial independence have had the added effect of delaying marriage. Because a woman's financial security no longer depends on the man she marries, the pressure is off, and many women give themselves the time to live with their partners before making the big commitment. Our emotional needs, however, have not evolved at the same rate. Whether we want to admit it or not, most of us women are still on a mission to tie down our man.

Despite the rise of cohabitation, we haven't seen a whole generation shun marriage and stick to being just housemates. Actually, far from it. It's just that now cohabitation is seen as a dry run for marriage. They say that you never really know someone until you've lived with him, so living together has become the ultimate test for those who are planning marriage for the future.

Surprisingly, couples who live together for more than two years before they marry tend to divorce faster, suggesting there is a finite "trial period" before living together should become marriage. We all know of couples who lived together for years and were blissfully happy *until* married.

But whether you and your partner view moving in together as the next step before naming the date and picking the rings, as an alternative to making the big commitment, or as an entirely separate issue from marriage, it is still a huge step in any relationship. Motives, expectations, and actual experiences will vary for every individual and every relationship. Living together will bring up a whole heap of questions that you should think seriously about. Why do you want to move in together? Do you share the same motives, or do you have different reasons for the move? Are you viewing the experience as a prelude to marriage while he sees it as a long-term end in itself? What are your expectations? Are you dreaming of decorating your new home together while he is already planning his first poker night in—pizza and beer included?

WHY MAKE THE MOVE?

When the living-together issue arises, it usually means a relationship has reached the stage when the couple wants to spend more time together. Often couples also move in for financial or logistical reasons. As with Alice and Richard at the beginning of the chapter, it seems silly paying for two apartments when you're spending so much time together or if one of you lives on the other side of town and thus getting together involves lots of traveling. And as always, our exact motives are shaped by whether we are a woman or a man.

For an example of why men and women view cohabitation differently, just look back as far as your own childhood. To this day, many women remember playing with dollhouses and mini baking sets. And the boys? Were they baking scrumptious cakes made out of imaginary ingredients? No way! They were too busy running around the yard with action figures, saving the world. Even today, most women are conditioned to be homemakers from childhood. We're taught that a cozy home is something to strive for. How many domestic-type magazines are marketed to men? Men are taught to see home as somewhere to sleep and hang out.

How many of your boyfriend's childhood heroes were house proud? It's unlikely that James Bond stopped in at Bed Bath & Beyond to grab some lavender-scented linen spray after a hard day of spying.

It's no coincidence that most male heroes live alone. Even the language to describe someone living alone is loaded. When a woman lives alone she is a sad old spinster, but a man who lives alone is described as a fun-loving bachelor. It's clear to see why men and women would view cohabitation differently.

Lisa and Barry are both in their late twenties. They've been together for two years and both pay ridiculously high rent on their respective apartments. Barry's lease is coming up for renewal, so Lisa suggests that he should move into her place. To Lisa, this is a natural progression. After all, they spend pretty much every night together anyway, and it seems illogical for her to lug her clothes to his apartment every night. Lisa's fairly convinced that she and Barry will go the distance and eventually get married. It makes perfect sense that they would take that next step and start sharing living space. Except that when she suggests this to Barry, he goes strangely quiet and proceeds to spend the next six nights out with the boys. Confused, she takes it up with him:

> LISA: Have you thought any more about us moving in together?

Lisa meant *Why are you avoiding the issue? What's the big deal here?*

Barry heard *Give me an answer NOW. Are you going to let me move in and rule your life or not?*

BARRY: Why rush things? It will work itself out naturally.

Lisa heard *I'm not that serious about the relationship.*

LISA: When will you grow up? There's no point in this relationship if it's not going to move forward.

Barry heard *Move in with me or it's over.*

BARRY: (*I won't be bullied into letting her make all my decisions. I'll put this off some more and deal with it next week. I'm going out for a drink.*)

What's happening here is that Barry perceives a sudden threat to his independence. The relationship is great, he is serious about her, and he has no interest in leaving her for anybody else. But the mention of moving in brings with it thoughts of marriage and being tied down, and that is too much for Barry to handle. Thus he hears her suggestion as nagging and views it as an attempt to trap him into something he's not ready for. Since Lisa thinks moving in together is a positive step, Barry's resistance is seen as him not liking her and not wanting to be in the relationship. Of course, neither of these perceptions is correct, but the way we are socialized means that Lisa is likely to feel more positively about these levels of commitment and Barry is more likely to associate them with loss and restriction.

GREAT EXPECTATIONS

Unfortunately, the potential for conflict doesn't end as soon as you've made that crucial initial decision to move in together. Oh no, because moving in with a partner is a big deal. If a couple decides to bite the bullet and go for it, chances are they've both put a great deal of thought into it. And in turn, this means that they've probably got very definite expectations about what living together will be like. And while you're picturing candlelit dinner parties, he's wondering if the extra bedroom can be made into a game room.

Of course our happiness with our living setup doesn't just come from meeting our own expectations; it also comes from having expectations that are similar to those of our partner. If you and your partner are expecting hugely different things from living together, somewhere along the line, one or both of you are going to be let down.

But why would two people of similar age and similar interests have such varying views on how a romantic love nest should operate? Well, once again the home you grew up in colors your view of how you would like your own home to be, from small issues such as whether or not you remove your shoes at the door to how much privacy people should give one another. Plus, our views on conflict resolution, division of labor, and closeness are all shaped by our early and unique experiences of living at home.

Some families place emphasis on openly discussing problems, while others encourage avoiding conflict altogether. If your boyfriend grew up in a house where his mom did all the housework, he won't be used to getting his hands dirty doing "woman's" work. Because our childhood home is the first environment we familiarize ourselves with, the lessons we learn here can stick for life.

Sidney and Anita have just moved in together. Sidney comes from a very traditional Greek family. His mother takes great pride in caring for her four sons and husband and relishes the cooking, cleaning, and fussing it entails. On the other hand, Anita was raised by her mother, an endlessly busy career woman who returned to work as soon as her two kids were old enough to walk back from school on their own. The trouble here is that Anita was taught by her upbringing that the best way to ensure you get fed and have a clean house is to do it yourself. Which works fine, apart from Sidney, who is left starving on the sofa waiting for someone to clear his lunch plate and make him some dinner.

SIDNEY: Darling, what's for dinner?

ANITA: (*Why are you asking me? You know where the kitchen is.*) I haven't even thought about it.

SIDNEY: (*She's too busy to make time for me. I thought that when a woman loves you, she wanted to take care of you.*) Oh, I thought, as the woman of the house, you would be all over that.

Anita heard *I expect you to do everything in the house.*

ANITA: You're not living with your mother anymore.

Sidney heard *I disagree with the way you were brought up, you big mommy's boy!*

Sidney and Anita will have to find a compromise that takes into account how their vastly different upbringings have shaped two equally different sets of expectations. The pressures and duties of everyday life mean that a couple newly living together will have to deal with issues they've never come across before. So, if your boyfriend comes from a family where Mom sorted the finances, while your father always paid the bills, then you need to discuss how you compromise the expectations you may have of each other, preferably before the electricity gets cut off.

When we don't get this compromise right, the results can be disastrous. When a man says, "But I want to go watch the game with the guys. It's my life and I can do what I want," his girlfriend might hear "I don't care if this upsets you. My commitment is to my friends, not to my home with you." Equally when a woman says, "Would you mind doing the dishes tonight?" her boyfriend might not hear one word. He switched off the minute he realized he was being asked to perform a household chore and immediately reverted back to the thirteen-year-old who had to be bribed to wash the dishes!

Clearly there are elements of living together that need to be negotiated. Moving in represents an important transition stage for the relationship, where new boundaries need to be established and communicated.

MOVING IN AND MOVING FORWARD

No couple should despair if they are having problems adjusting to living with each other. Seeing your boyfriend four nights a week when you are in a good mood and wearing matching underwear is a whole different kettle of fish from seeing your boyfriend every time you want to chill out at home, every time you want to watch something different on TV, and every time you want to put on a face mask. And really, that's just scratching the surface. Moving in together presents a host of problems that you could never have dreamed would cause a rift. But this doesn't mean you can't work through them.

You need to set some boundaries from the very beginning. *Moving in with your partner means joining together your lives.* You find yourself having to make joint decisions about things like who buys the coffee and who has which side of the bed. It's best to confront the major issues through detailed conversations right from the start. Couples who do not plan these things in advance risk running into conflict at a later date.

You need to be realistic. When couples first date there is a tendency to idealize each other and mentally gloss over any differences. But the reality of living together will not live up to the fantasy you imagined during those first flushes of new love. And when our expectations are dashed and we begin arguing over the minutiae of living together, we can fall into the guilt-blame trap with our partner. But accepting the realities of a situation can actually provide the opportunity to get to know each other as real people and develop the relationship in the process.

TROUBLESHOOTING

To make living together as smooth as possible it's a good idea to identify potential trouble spots within your relationship and look at how you can cope with these situations when they occur.

Problem: Perceived insensitivity

Solution: Next time your partner says something like "I'm not ready to let you into my life to the point where we actually live together," before resorting to anger or insults, try to identify where your partner's feelings are coming from. Perhaps his last girlfriend tried to control his life the minute they swapped door keys. Maybe his father left the family home when he was very young and he is anxious that he might do the same. Resist the temptation to assume "My boyfriend won't let me move in because he is selfish" and acknowledge that these feelings are usually signs of hidden vulnerabilities or soft spots.

Problem: Biased thinking

Solution: Again, this looks at your ability to reflect on what your partner says to you. The easiest thing in the world is reacting to a comment or a situation as we immediately perceive it. But the most *useful* thing in the world is being able to remove yourself from the situation and obtain a far more neutral view, or even better, to be able to empathize with your partner and appreciate why he feels the way he does.

In romantic relationships, misinterpretation is the biggest cause of conflict. If your partner says, "I'm going out again tonight. I'll try not to wake you when I come in," instead of hearing "I'll be late. I can't be bothered to see you," make the effort to hear the sentiments intended. He more likely means "I love living with you, but I need to maintain relationships outside of ours. However, I accept that now we live together and my actions affect you, so I will try to be as quiet as I can if it is late when I come home."

You need to look at both your partner's and your own automatic thoughts and examine them for bias. Analyze your feelings and ask yourself if they are entirely justified, or if your feelings are influenced by factors that are unrelated to your partner's words or actions.

Problem: Resolving conflict

Solution: When conflict arises, change your tactics. Typically, we go into arguments with the aim of *winning*. Essentially we end up in a scenario that resembles two bulls locking horns. A far more effective strategy involves changing the objective, so you and your partner aren't battling to win the argument. Instead, you are working together to reach a compromise. Resolution, not retribution, should be the goal. You need to be able to discuss these issues without trying to score points. Winning an argument brings no satisfaction if it leaves your partner destroyed and your relationship in tatters. If you don't want to move in but your partner does, don't make your aim "I must keep going until I get my way and my partner accepts that I will never move in with him." Instead your mission statement should be "I recognize that my partner and I have conflicting views on this, and we will keep discussing it until we reach a solution that addresses and fulfils both sets of needs, so we can support each other."

Problem: Inability to make shared decisions

Solution: Making tricky decisions with your partner is like practicing a sport. The more you do it, the easier it becomes. Once you and your partner get into the routine of discussing issues, recognizing each other's points of view, and deciding on a clear path of action, it will become as much a part of your relationship as your sex life or Sunday-morning pancakes.

Problem: Expecting too much

Solution: Be realistic about what living with your partner will be like. Many of the difficulties in your relationship will still be present even after you decide to move in together. Sharing a roof won't whitewash your relationship and make it perfect. That doesn't mean that you can't work through your problems, it just means that you shouldn't expect cohabiting to solve them. Otherwise, you are likely to be disappointed down the line. The aim should be to set your own realistic goals and to discuss them with your partner. It is important to consider whether your goals are similar to his or else you could run into problems as your future together progresses. Be careful not to let wishful thinking or mind-reading get in the way of effective communication of your hopes and fears for your relationship. And ensure that you communicate with your partner on how you see cohabiting working to avoid your expectations being dashed once the boxes are unpacked and the bedroom set is already on its way.

MAKING IT WORK

The main thing to remember about moving in together is that most of the time your partner's not consciously being difficult or unloving. He's just being a man, or she's just being a woman. The more you talk about how you think and feel in a calm way, the closer you'll get to coming to a solution that makes you both happy.

Nadine and Franklin have been dating for two years and recently started the process of moving in together. One night, they get into a heated debate:

> NADINE: Please turn the TV off. I gathered some catalogs and we need to start looking at sofas.
>
> FRANKLIN: Game's on. Can we talk about it later?
>
> NADINE: Why don't you ever want to be more involved? Turn the TV off!
>
> FRANKLIN: No! Stop pestering me!
>
> NADINE: Don't make me feel like your mother! I'm so fed up with this.
>
> FRANKLIN: Pick out whatever sofa you want. I'm going to watch the game at the bar.

Imagine how differently the conversation could have gone if Franklin had explained his feelings a little more and Nadine had dwelled on hers a little less.

> NADINE: Are you busy? I wanted to get your opinion on what sofa we should buy.
>
> FRANKLIN: Can we talk a little later? I want to watch the end of this game. I know we do need to make a decision, though.
>
> NADINE: No problem.

It's important to be careful about putting your partner in a role he or she doesn't want to be in. No one wants to be the naughty child or the chastising mother, but by interacting in a way that minimizes the person down to a specific behavior, we find ourselves shoved into those types of roles. This of course only serves to escalate the problem. With a few simple changes to her opener, Nadine manages to change the tone from accusatory to light. She makes the discussion feel like a joint decision, not one she has made already, and she doesn't encroach on Franklin's personal time. In return, Franklin feels consulted, not confronted, and the conversation ends on a positive note.

Everyone who lives with someone else must go through a period of adjustment, and just because you and your partner love each other and want to spend the rest of your lives together, this doesn't exclude you. Make sure you keep talking. Nothing is so scary that it can't be reduced to a manageable size by a good long chat with your loved one.

And beyond talking, make sure you listen. Not to what you want to hear, not even to what your partner is actually saying (although that's a good start), but to what your partner is trying to say. Put yourself in his position. Leave your own judgments at the door, and the two of you will likely develop a routine that will benefit your relationship long after the housewarming party.

TIPS TO REMEMBER

- Reframe cohabitation for your man. Make it about gaining intimacy and fun, rather than losing freedom and space.
- Don't overanalyze. Learn to accept that sometimes what your man says is what he means.
- Have realistic expectations. This doesn't mean not being positive, but it does mean getting rid of the script that you have in your head about how everything MUST proceed.

CHAPTER 9

Fighting Fair

Sarah and Ben have been married for five years. They have two children and recently moved into a bigger house to accommodate their growing family.

> SARAH: Ben, it's so great that you leave your dirty clothes on the floor. How else would I know which ones to clean?

> BEN: How about I pick them up after I've paid these bills you were supposed to take care of. You know, you don't actually have to wait until they're red to pay them.

> SARAH: Well, perhaps if I got more help around the house and with the kids, I might have time to do everything else.

BEN: With the money we'd save on late fees, you could pay for twelve maids.

SARAH: What are you saying? I don't clean the house properly?

BEN: Walked right into that one, didn't you?

The most common things couples argue about are money, sex, work, children, and housework. These areas have lots of potential to cause arguments within a relationship. Some deal with the ordinary everyday stuff like who takes out the garbage and whose turn it is to wash the dishes. Financial responsibilities fall under this area too.

Like most things that have to do with male-female communication, if you want to see what a fight is really about, you need to look a little deeper. In Sarah and Ben's case, on the surface it might appear to be about who does the washing and how the bills are getting paid. Yet Sarah quite possibly feels Ben is being disrespectful to her. When Ben talks about her paying her bills, what he's really doing is expressing his deep-seated fear about falling into debt and losing their house. If they really knew what the other was thinking, they would be able to reassure each other and talk about their fears without bickering.

When agitated and angry, we are a lot less likely to take a deep breath and try to reason things out. We rarely focus on what we are really thinking and instead concentrate only on the anger bubbling up. To complicate things further, the issues that annoy us often are rooted in our views about the world and our ability to tolerate different levels of discomfort or anxiety. What is clean for one person may be considered an unbearable mess for another. If your mom made it clear while you were growing up that a messy bedroom meant you were being lazy, disrespecting the home, and not taking care of your responsibilities, then you are going to have a very different attitude than the guy whose mom did everything for him because he was her little prince and caring for him was the way she showed love.

Lucy adores Paul and thinks they have a great relationship. He's funny, kind, and always surprising her with little poems and gifts. Paul loves Lucy, too. She's very successful at her job, smarter than any other girl he's dated, fantastic looking, and has an amazing apartment. The problems arise when he moves in with her and, funnily enough, she doesn't cook, clean, or do his laundry.

> PAUL: Great, takeout again. At least it keeps that brand-new oven all shiny and clean, which is more than can be said for the bedroom. When was the last time you changed the sheets?

> LUCY: If you want a home-cooked meal, don't let me stop you. And the sheets were changed last Friday. If you don't like it, change them yourself.

> PAUL: I never knew any girl who did less cooking and cleaning than you. It's bizarre.

> LUCY: Welcome to the twenty-first century! I'm not cooking and cleaning for you.

> PAUL: Well, what exactly are you bringing to this

relationship? Because you don't seem to care about me at all.

What is this fight really about? First off, all her life Lucy witnessed her mother slaving over a hot stove and being treated like a servant by the rest of her family. Lucy vowed not to be like this and wants to be the breadwinner, paying someone else to do the cleaning and cooking she hates. Paul's mom waited on him hand and foot. She showed her love by cooking his favorite chicken dish and making sure clean shirts and socks appeared magically in his drawers. How can the two of them address this conflict and get to the bottom of their fight?

Paul needs to ask himself why it's so important that Lucy cooks and cleans for him. Is he really asking her for a demonstration of her love and affection for him? If this is the case, could she express it on her own terms by maybe treating him to a meal out, giving him a cuddle, or simply reassuring him that she loves him?

On the other hand, would it kill Lucy to surprise Paul with the occasional mac 'n' cheese? It wouldn't mean that she was reducing herself to being a maid, and it would send a message to Paul about the way she felt about him in a language Paul was familiar with from childhood.

As stated earlier, most conflicts fall under a few major categories. Since those everyday arguments may conceal deeper meanings, we need to learn how to clarify what the conflict is. It's a matter of defining the problem and then working together to discover a solution.

SOURCES OF CONFLICT

Housework

When it comes to arguments that revolve around the basic tasks of getting through day-to-day life, often just sitting and talking about what *messy* and *neat* really means to you will work much better than screaming at him to pick up his pants and telling him you feel he is insulting you when he expects you to pick up after him. He is more likely to respond to the meanings you ascribe to his behavior rather than an angry rant. And of course try to take into account his views. If he says he is happy to do his share of the housework but needs some downtime when he comes home from work before he pitches in, don't make the heap of dishes in the sink the first topic of conversation when he gets home. Simply coming up with a chore list together—not one that is dictated by one person and carried out by the other—is a great way of really talking about things and working through who does what. Just make sure that you both feel it's fair and make a pact to keep to it. Ultimately housework is relatively easy to sort out. It comes down to respecting each other's needs, each other's boundaries, and each other enough to make the time to talk about the things that really bother you.

Money

On the face of it, the issue of money is not that different from the issue of housework. After all, it is about attitudes: the way that you see the role that money plays in your life and what money should be used for (fun, savings, charity). For both men and women, this generally reflects the values that we were taught as children. Growing up in a household where "Waste not, want not" was the motto is going to have a different effect on you than if the family motto was "Go for it! You only live once!" If you share the same attitude about the *value* of money, there really isn't much of a problem.

Issues of gender *do* come into play when one person seems to hold more economic power than the other. In our society, money is one of the strongest indicators of power, so in a relationship the person who has more may see himself or herself (or be seen by the other partner) as contributing more or having more value in the relationship. This can be especially sticky when gender stereotypes are reversed. For example, a man who makes less than his wife may feel that his masculinity is being challenged. Consequently, when she asks him to help with the dishes, his reaction may be overly defensive to ensure that his masculinity is not threatened further. Likewise, if the wife is put in the position where she doesn't get involved with or even know much about the household finances, then her contribution to the relationship may feel minimized and she may back down from asserting her opinion.

In most cases a successful relationship is one where both people feel equal and feel they can exert the same influence. This doesn't mean that both need to bring home the same paycheck. It means they are both able to see money as just one of the many ways a person can contribute to a relationship.

Intimacy

Issues that center on intimacy include being too tired for sex or having different ways of showing affection. Sex, like most things in a relationship, changes over time. That doesn't mean that it gets worse; it just changes. Doing it on the kitchen floor was great when you first met, but when you are trying to make toast, resynch your BlackBerry, and clean out the week-old cat litter box, it's just not going to happen. The important thing to remember is that even though life gets in the way of sex, it is still very important to make time for it. Interestingly, sex isn't something that most of us actually "argue" about. It's usually what we *don't* say that leads to festering resentment about how little we're getting or the quality of it. That's why it's important to learn to talk about what you like. It's worth getting past vocabulary that makes you cringe just so you can get what you desire from each other. Don't expect him to mind-read and just *know* what you want. Nip conflict in the bud by opening up the lines of communication straightaway.

But don't just talk the talk . . . you need to make time for sex! Vegging in front of the TV every night until one of you is snoring won't help. It takes work to cultivate a good sex life. Setting a date every week might feel contrived, but it won't once it becomes a good habit. Think quality, not quantity. When you go for it really enjoy it and indulge. Play out your fantasies and really let go. It's a good way to ensure everybody's happiness.

ARGUMENTS: THE DEEPER ISSUES

Heather and Darren are looking at houses. They have three
young kids and have decided they need to move to a bigger
house in the suburbs. Heather has her heart set on a big
house with a big backyard, but the only ones in their price
range are farther from the city.

> HEATHER: But I thought you liked the last house
> we saw. It had five bedrooms and a big backyard
> for the kids to play in.
>
> DARREN: It was too sprawling—too much up-
> keep.
>
> HEATHER: But wasn't that the whole point? We
> need more space, and it could be a project we
> could do together.
>
> DARREN: Maybe we should stay in the city. We're
> comfy and it's nice having everything so close.
>
> HEATHER: But there is not enough room and
> we've always dreamed of living in the suburbs.
>
> DARREN: No, it's where *you* always dreamed of
> living.

Your beliefs and ideals can be huge battlegrounds. If
someone challenges your fundamental ideas, like what is
the right balance between work and play or whether you
should live in the city or the suburbs, it can feel as if you are
being attacked directly.

These are some of the more central issues that we need to navigate in a relationship. Arguments here often occur because people are so dogmatic about their view they refuse to see anyone else's. It is important to recognize that many times these views are bound up in how we view ourselves. For example, Heather's thinking error could be "Living in the city is fine when it was just us, but I am only a good mother if my kids grow up with a big backyard to play in." But Darren's might be "It's my duty as a good father to provide, but I can only do that if I live in a big city, near my office."

Once the ideas and beliefs behind the arguments are visible, couples like Heather and Darren are more able to see each other's point of view. It promotes understanding and allows the couple to come to some sort of compromise. Heather could have a house not quite as large closer to the city, and Darren can be a little farther from the city but still within a reasonable commute. The thing is that before we get to the point that we can compromise, we need to be honest with our partners and, more importantly, with ourselves about what the real issues are.

Unfortunately even understanding the real issues at hand is not always enough. The way we choose to communicate these issues can often get in the way. If the method in which you argue affects the way you understand and empathize with each other's point of view, you will have an even more difficult time reaching a compromise.

Jessica and Sean are in the process of redoing their kitchen. They are both becoming increasingly anxious, as it is costing more than they originally thought. Sean wanted to wait and not do everything at once, but Jessica insisted that they do everything now, since it will save money in the long run. Sean gave in and now frustration is running high:

JESSICA: You always blow everything out of proportion.

SEAN: I knew it would all go wrong if we didn't get the details right! But you had to rush right in.

JESSICA: Well, I knew it would end up with me doing everything! I called the contractor, I picked out the tile, I decided on the new stove. If you knew it would go wrong, why not say something?

SEAN: You're such a control freak; you had to do it all your way! I said from the get-go we were taking on too much!

In most cases an argument is sparked off simply because we aren't taking the time to listen and understand the other person's point of view. Even smaller conflicts can take on life-or-death proportions when both sides get frustrated at the lack of understanding from the other side. Jessica and Sean's argument is exaggerated to make a point, but we're all guilty of using "all-or-nothing" statements in arguments, making sweeping assumptions about the situation and then maximizing the negatives. Even if we think we don't agree with our partner, if we don't listen properly in the first place, how will we really know if we agree or not? In most situations a conflict is only resolved when we are able to use communication and negotiation to work out a compromise. At no time is this need to *really* listen to each other and communicate more critical than when we are faced with one of life's big changes. Happy or sad, major life events—births, marriage, infidelity, illness, and death—always shake us up and make arguments much more likely. Such events challenge our ability to cope with change and with the unexpected.

As life changes we need to adapt not only as individuals but also as a couple. There may be times when we feel we are protecting each other from pain by isolating ourselves, but it is at these times when we really need to let our guard down. Some core tips for dealing with arguments that stem from a major life change are:

- If possible try not to focus only on the negative effects of change.
- See if there are some positives to be derived from the situation.
- Don't displace your hurt, anger, or grief onto your partner.
- Remember, you are in it together.
- Separate your emotions from practical tasks and conflicts.

Whatever the reason you are arguing, whether it's a simple tiff about whose turn it is to take out the garbage or a full-blown shouting match about how rude he is around your parents, it is important to figure out why you are really arguing and to deal with the *real* problem at hand. Like any crisis, couple arguments need to be dealt with both emotionally and practically. So work through the feelings, but also make the practical changes necessary to ensure that you actually reach some resolution. The argument is the jumping-off point. Once you both have established there is a problem, make it less about personal attacks and more about why you are feeling the way you are. Arguments about what time you should leave to meet friends for drinks probably have a deeper meaning than your personal philosophy on departure times. An argument about how much television your two-year-old should be allowed to watch may be about your own personal fears of not being a good parent. But until you disclose what is truly upsetting you—to your partner and yourself—you can't begin to resolve the problem at hand.

Some couples seem to argue about the same things over and over again. Or as soon as they have resolved one conflict, another arises. It's important to look out for unhelpful conflict patterns that may prevent the two of you from getting to the bottom of and eventually putting an end to the argument. The big problem with finding a resolution comes back to a recurring issue: He's a man, you're a woman.

This may come as no surprise, but men and women argue differently. Men have a tendency to bottle up their feelings during arguments with their partners. The notion that the more a woman pursues a topic or harasses her husband about it, the more he withdraws is not new. In fact, many psychologists refer to this as the "nag-withdraw cycle." As she tries to get to the bottom of things, he backs off, and when he backs off she feels the need to talk more. This argument dynamic often becomes more important than the topic of dispute, causing added tension and stopping the couple from addressing the actual disagreement.

COMMON CONFLICT ERRORS

It's important to be aware of the following common conflict errors that get in the way of really resolving the issue at hand.

Old Baggage

Simon has planned a night out at a fancy restaurant for Zoe, his wife of two years. Reservations are hard to get. Simon has planned this night for a few weeks, but now Zoe can't make it.

> SIMON: You do this every single time.
>
> ZOE: What?
>
> SIMON: Every time I plan a night out, you "forget" and can't make it.
>
> ZOE: My mom isn't well. I promised I'd drop by and cook her dinner. Surely you don't begrudge me a night with my mom. We can go out anytime.
>
> SIMON: No, we can't. I know you'll be busy the next time I arrange something special. Everything's ruined.

Memories about betrayal or neglect earlier in life can be triggered in arguments without partners realizing it, and so instead of responding to the real issue at hand, you respond to the old baggage you've been carrying around. Let's take a closer look at what's going on with Simon and Zoe:

SIMON: You do this every single time.

Simon is giving a classic "all-or-nothing" statement to Zoe about her actions.

ZOE: What?

SIMON: Every time I plan a night out, you "forget" and can't make it.

He's mind reading and making it personal, assuming she purposely forgot because she doesn't take his feelings into consideration.

ZOE: My mom isn't well. I promised I'd drop by and cook her dinner. Surely you don't begrudge me a night with my mom. We can go out anytime.

Now Zoe's mind reading, assuming Simon is trying to stop her from seeing her mom.

SIMON: No, we can't. I know you'll be busy the next time I arrange something special. Now everything's ruined.

He's taking the mind reading to another level, assuming she's making excuses not to see him, and making the situation catastrophic—"everything's ruined."

What's really going on here? Simon's father left the family home when he was nine years old. His father often let him down at the last minute on visitation days. Simon's mother would get very agitated and upset about it in front of Simon. Simon's core belief became "If you cancel a date with me,

it means that you don't love me and don't want to see me."
Zoe is pretty relaxed about rearranging dates and doesn't
understand Simon's anxiety and seeming overreaction. If
she knew that Simon equated the date change with being
rejected, she would be able to handle the situation more
sympathetically. If Simon was aware his reaction was based
on old baggage, not the actual situation, he might be able to
handle it in a calmer, more logical fashion.

Ticking Time Bombs

We all have them, those events in a relationship that really
hurt us or affected our trust in our partner. We may have addressed these stories but don't feel they are really resolved,
like the time he forgot to pick you up from the airport or the
day he overheard you telling a friend that you hated visiting
his parents. It may even be the almost affair he had with the
redhead in payroll. The point is, before we forgive and forget
we really need to make sure we are ready to forgive and forget. That means talking about things and not burying them
to convince ourselves that all is OK again. If we do, we will
only end up resenting our partners, and those buried memories will turn into time bombs waiting to explode.

Camouflaging

As we've seen, in a lot of cases the arguments that people
have are not really the arguments that they want to have.
It's easier to scream and shout about the way he leaves his
clothes all over the bathroom floor than to sit down and
address the issue that you feel devalued in the relationship. We use safe, camouflaged topics because it's easier. Of

course this prevents us from resolving the real underlying issues.

Keeping the Peace at the Risk of Resolution

This happens when a person hates conflict and will do anything to avoid it. The problem here is this person's own needs often take a backseat to everyone else's and their opinions rarely get heard. This then leads to resentment and possible passive-aggressive behavior.

Kill or Be Killed (A Little Dramatic But You Get the Picture)

You are more focused on winning the argument than getting to a fair and healthy resolution of the issue, so you go in with guns blazing, take cheap shots, and usually scare your partner into going along with what you say. This leads to your partner feeling as if he hasn't been heard or, worse yet, feeling unable to tell you how he feels, which means that by the time the argument is over, you haven't resolved a thing.

Playing the Guessing Game

This is where you want to make your feelings known but you want to make your partner work for the privilege of figuring out what's wrong. It's a way of punishing him. You go quiet, bang kitchen cupboards, and give one-syllable answers until he notices things aren't quite right. You may eventually get to the point of sharing what is really wrong, but by that time you are both so exhausted and confused that negotiating a resolution is much harder.

The Historian

This is where you bring up the whole history of the relationship rather than focusing on the issue at hand. It usually puts the other person's back against the wall and makes him defensive, which will make it harder for you to get your point across. If you really want to bring up a "relationship pattern" that you have a problem with rather than a specific issue, you need to address it as such and not dredge up things that happened in the summer of '98 to make your point.

The Drama Major

This is much more of a female trait. Tears and big gasps of disbelief followed by the slamming of doors is an unfair way for someone to passive-aggressively withdraw from a situation. Her partner is left feeling guilty but simultaneously cheated from the opportunity to resolve the issue, and this kind of behavior can lead to feelings of resentment and double standards.

These are the things you should *not* do when attempting to fight fair. But what are you actually supposed to do in an argument? Well, the majority of disagreements within a relationship are about power and control. Just like brokering peace in the Middle East, it's not useful to go down the road of tit for tat. Instead you need to learn to negotiate.

1. **Listen calmly to your partner's viewpoint.** Make sure you actually hear what is being said. A great way of doing this is simply to ask—"When you said it feels like you have too much on your plate, I heard that you felt I wasn't there to help you out with things. Is that what you mean?"

2. Own what you say. Begin statement with "I feel" rather than "You make me feel."

3. Learn to empathize. Being able to see things from his point of view will make it easier for you to communicate with him.

4. Be aware of your own thinking errors. Are you really arguing about the household finances or is there a deeper issue that you need to address?

5. Be self-aware. The more you are aware of how your behavior affects him, the more you can look at ways to modify it to bring about the solution you want.

6. Be aware of your tone. The more defensive or aggressive you come across, the more likely you will both stop listening to each other.

7. Take turns. Remember conflict resolution is all about collaboration.

8. Compromise. It is not about winning the argument; it is about fairly resolving the issue.

9. At the end, remember to repair. Apologize if you feel you have hurt each other in any way, comment on the positives that you think came out of the argument, and let it go.

It would be very weird not to have disagreements, arguments, and conflict in a relationship between two healthy adults with minds and lives of their own. These are not signs of dysfunction, but of two normal people struggling to be heard and trying to get their own needs met while keeping their partner happy. If handled correctly, conflict can have a constructive, not destructive, effect on relationships, and there is nothing more fun then making up after a good fight.

TIPS TO REMEMBER

- In an argument, it's very rare that anyone sets out deliberately to hurt his or her partner—it's usually a defense or anxiety that causes hurtful words.
- Listen to what the argument is really about.
- Don't try to "win" an argument. It should always be about compromise and resolution.

CHAPTER 10

When He (or You) Cheats

Samantha and Peter recently celebrated their three-year wedding anniversary. But all is not right, and Samantha is worried. Peter seems distant and distracted, and he has worked late for three straight nights. Yet when she called him at the office, she got no answer.

> SAMANTHA: But there are texts from her on your phone, you've worked late three times this week, and you definitely smell of perfume. Come *on*, Peter, I'm not stupid!

> PETER: Nothing happened. She's just a friend. Her husband treats her really badly; she needs someone to talk to.

> SAMANTHA: Well, what about me? I need someone to talk to as well, and you're my husband, supposedly.

PETER: What's that supposed to mean?

SAMANTHA: You're never here. I never get to see you.

PETER: Well, perhaps I'd be around more if you were nicer to be with. All you do is complain and watch television. It's not exactly exciting times.

SAMANTHA: Well, excuse *me* for just being normal. Relationships can't be passionate and thrilling all the time. This isn't Hollywood, you know!

Whatever way you look at it, infidelity, whether physical or emotional, is one of the biggest emotional crises that can affect a relationship. If it happens in your relationship, learning to handle it is crucial. It's a hot topic, and very controversial. What constitutes cheating? Is thinking about cheating as bad as committing the act? Does a kiss count? Have you been unfaithful the minute you fail to mention that you are in a relationship? And what is the best way to deal with infidelity? How many strikes do you get before you're out? Can a relationship ever recover from any type of infidelity? Is a leopard capable of changing his spots?

Cheating is still one of the big players when it comes to relationship strife, and it causes huge emotional turmoil. Jealousy, resentment, lack of intimacy, power plays, cruelty, and fighting for your needs to be met all come up when one or both partners decide to stray. And the different genders have completely different ideas about what infidelity is and how to deal with it.

Surprise, surprise, in every crumbling relationship you

will find our old friend lack of communication at the heart of the problem. If we could truly connect with our partner and know exactly what each other's needs are and what every fight really means, then affairs would probably never happen.

Affairs by definition are hidden and secretive. Sure there are those ecstatically content couples who delight in the joys of an open relationship, but most occurrences of sex outside an exclusive relationship are rarely openly tolerated. Extramarital sex is the most common reason for divorce in nearly every country and culture in the world. Around 70 percent of marriages will have to deal with infidelity at some point. And whereas affairs have previously been seen as the domain of men with "lipstick on their collar," adultery has now become almost as prevalent among women as it is among men.

One of the common misconceptions about infidelity is that it is the first step in the downfall of an otherwise healthy relationship. Actually, an affair or a betrayal is more likely to be a symptom of existing problems and a warning sign, as opposed to a sudden and unexpected blow to the relationship. If a partner is cheating, it's likely that there are already problems within the relationship. Essentially, affairs tend not to occur within a genuinely happy partnership; rather than being a *catalyst* of problems, they are usually an *indicator.*

While the betrayal itself may evoke feelings of rejection and unleash the equivalent of a firing squad on your self-esteem (if you even get your head around the fact that your partner may have committed a physical betrayal), what often goes on to destroy a relationship is the fear that it may happen again, coupled with the behavior that this fear is likely to produce. How can we stop the damage from totally destroying a relationship? How can we look beyond these immediate responses and make sure (a) we understand *why* it happened in the first place and (b) how the relationship can come back from it? First we need to ask some searching questions:

WHY DOES IT HAPPEN?

There are two universal truths when it comes to affairs. First, whatever he or she tells you, affairs don't "just happen." They don't occur out of the blue. Second, affairs simply do not happen when a relationship is happy, well founded, and healthy. When both partners feel fulfilled by and contented with the relationship, an affair is very unlikely. There are specific relationship variables that are closely linked to infidelity and can help explain why it occurs in the first place.

1. Lack of relationship satisfaction. One of the most obvious explanations of infidelity is a change in the state of the relationship or a continuing lack of relationship quality. Women dissatisfied within a marriage are more likely to cheat than men are. This may be because men are more motivated to cheat by factors such as opportunity, rather than by deep-seated, ongoing motivations.

Marital satisfaction can be broken down into factors such as sexual satisfaction, quality of emotional support, and the level of love and affection experienced in the relationship. The sexual side of a relationship is usually much more important to a man, while women often cite emotional issues as central to marital discord. Jealousy, possessiveness, condescension, and withholding sex are common causes of adultery. For example, a man overly worried about his spouse's fidelity will show high levels of jealousy and possessiveness and perhaps belittle in an effort to lower his partner's self-esteem. Yet his actions will make his spouse look for contentment outside the marriage, and a self-perpetuating cycle is established.

Spouses who complain about their partners' flirting with others are also very likely to cheat themselves. They may be jealous that their spouse is giving sexual attention to someone else and decide to repay that behavior by being flirtatious or even having a one-night stand, no matter how harmless the original spouse's flirting may be. Sometimes they interpret innocuous behavior as flirty because of their own guilty conscience; they are projecting their own cheating thoughts on their innocent partner.

2. A coping mechanism. An affair can become a way of coping if the marriage is having problems. For someone who can't find the courage to end a marriage, having an affair provides the security and diversion of a new beginning, which can protect against and obscure the consequences of a divorce. It provides distraction from any painful feelings one may have about finishing a relationship. But our ability to face an ending head-on and cope with the ensuing emotional disruption is linked to our emotional intelligence and, inevitably, to our previous relationship experiences. Constantly turning to cheating as a method of avoiding endings is a sign that we have not developed this ability.

3. It's "hereditary." Infidelity is intricately linked to family patterns, in the same way that emotional unavailability, commitment problems, and sexual issues take cues from our early childhood experiences of relationships. Research shows that being unfaithful is almost hereditary! It's been said a million times here, but the relationships we observe as children teach us how to conduct ourselves within our own relationships. If we grow up in an atmosphere where Mom is continuously coming to terms with Dad's latest indiscretion, it is likely that we will accept this relationship model as normal and will go on to tolerate, initiate, or even expect infidelity.

4. It's a personality type. Some experts think that certain personality types are more likely to cheat. For example, people who are easily bored, have short attention spans, feel dissatisfied, or have low self-esteem are more likely to be unfaithful. No empirical research has been conducted to prove these hypotheses, however.

Interestingly, narcissism has also been highlighted as a strong predictor of susceptibility to infidelity; people who regard themselves as "special," who tend to be emotionally shallow and lack empathy, are more likely to stray. These findings also support the idea that infidelity can be a way to boost self-esteem and shore up a tender ego. A person who displays genuine self-confidence and self-esteem is unlikely to turn to an affair as a means of validation. Conversely, if an individual has low self-esteem, the excitement and flattery of an affair provides him with the ego-boost he so desperately requires.

Whatever the reasons or motivations, it does appear that people who are open to cheating, or even anticipate cheating, will cheat. Equally, if people do not have the right mindset for infidelity, it won't happen.

WHAT DOES THIS MEAN FOR BOTH OF YOU?

When infidelity occurs, a million different excuses will be given. Some are more plausible than others ("I was drunk and stupid" is always slightly more believable than "I slipped and fell on top of her"). For men, heading up the top ten get-out clauses is "It meant nothing, it was just sex." As we've already established, while sex may be "just sex" for a man, the phrase doesn't even exist in the vocabulary of most women. For women, it is rarely "just sex," because they tend to attach much more emotional meaning to the physical act. So, predictably, for women, the most common excuse is "I couldn't help it. I fell in love with him. He made me feel special and I couldn't resist." Thus, both genders try to justify the transgression using their specific view of sex. Ironically, the excuses given by each gender represent their own worse nightmare. For a man, the physical betrayal by his partner is more devastating to his psyche, while a woman is more hurt by the emotional infidelity exhibited by her man.

Frequently, affairs either make or break a relationship. Understanding the meaning of an affair makes it possible to unravel the real underlying issues. Since infidelity is usually a symptom of an unhealthy relationship, you must figure out why the affair happened and what it signals in terms of your relationship. When we cheat on a partner, we're not just cheating on him or her; we're usually covertly conveying one of a variety of messages. According to researchers who study couple dynamics, an affair can communicate any of the following messages:

1. I'll make you pay attention to me. This message is usually evident in couples who cannot talk about and resolve differences. Dissatisfactions are not aired and communication is limited in an effort to avoid conflict. This kind of affair is often a result of frustration combined with opportunity. Infidelity is likely to constitute a quick fling as opposed to a long-term affair, because ultimately, its express purpose is to command attention. Like a naughty child smacking his sibling in an attempt to get Mom's attention, this type of affair is designed to provoke.

2. I feel uncomfortable needing you so much. A fear of dependency pushes people to prove they can get their needs met elsewhere. This belief is often seen in couples who have problems with intimacy. Both spouses fear letting down the barriers and becoming emotionally vulnerable, and find it safer if a distance exists. For this couple, emotional connection is possibly achieved through fighting and conflict. The affair provides that conflict and consequently allows both partners to distance themselves from their genuine, intimidating emotions and protects them against hurt and disappointment.

3. Fill me up. Affairs provide ways of filling voids created by emotional emptiness. Partners who participate in affairs for this reason are likely to cheat with a string of sexual partners and enter into a number of different relationships. They look for fulfillment and validation and do not feel completed by their primary relationship. The message here is "You are not enough. This relationship is not enough. I need more."

4. I feel a duty to my partner, but I am in love with someone else. This is the underlying cry of individuals who remain in a relationship out of a sense of duty, in the name of doing "the right thing." This type of affair often arises when an individual has denied his or her emotional needs or when kids are involved. Often, the original relationship feels empty and communication is limited to practical matters, while the affair itself is a serious relationship that provides for the unmet emotional needs.

5. Help me leave my partner. A partner who is thinking about ending his or her current relationship may slide into an affair. These affairs act as trials to see if the person can make it on his or her own or if he or she is still attractive to the opposite sex. At the deeper level, this message also demonstrates a desire to avoid taking responsibility for ending the relationship.

Distinguishing among the various meanings is important as it can help predict the prognosis of the marriage. Rebuilding a relationship after infidelity may or may not be possible, depending on the infidelity's exact meanings. The future of your relationship will also be dependent on your emotional reaction to the indiscretion, and this of course is highly dependant on whether you are a man or a woman.

THE IMPACT OF INFIDELITY

If you haven't grasped the concept that men and women experience and express emotions differently by this stage in the book, then quite frankly, you haven't been paying attention! Of course there are similarities. That crushing moment when you realize the blond girl from work isn't just "a girl from work" or the moment when the link between your girlfriend's new underwear and your best friend's smug grin becomes painfully clear are universally awful. The big thing with infidelity is that it shatters our comfort zone and violates our expectations. Within a seemingly happy, healthy relationship we come to expect certain qualities and behaviors from our partner. We expect our partner to be honest, trustworthy, and respectful. Infidelity violates these fundamental assumptions. And this holds true for both men and women. But there are a number of aspects of infidelity that men and women deal with differently.

When we discover a partner has been unfaithful, one of the first things we will do is make an instant comparison between ourselves and the new object of our partner's affection. Usually we base these comparisons on what society teaches is of value for men and women. For women, of course, it's youth and beauty, so the question is usually "Is she younger than me?" or "Is she prettier than me?" For men it's money and status. Men are far more likely to envy social status and are more likely to feel jealous if their rival is more of an alpha male than they are.

However, comparison can also be more personal and based on the same factors we use as foundations for our own self-esteem. If we feel that much of our appeal as a mate arises from our intelligence, an immediate question will be "Is she smarter than I am?" Likewise, if an individual feels that one of her best traits is her sense of humor, she may well question "Does she make you laugh like I do?"

Consider this scenario. Leila has been going out with her boyfriend Jack for two years, and things are beginning to go stale. They have stopped making time for each other, and the relationship has slipped into a tired, boring routine. Meanwhile, Jack is becoming steadily closer to a girl at his gym. They've had dinner a few times, and gradually he finds himself confiding in her about his problems with Leila. No physical infidelity has occurred. On the other hand, after a Christmas party, Leila, high on festive spirit and red wine, finds herself passionately kissing a colleague. Now these two infidelities are completely different. Jack comforts himself with the fact that he hasn't cheated because he hasn't actually laid a finger on his gym buddy. Leila tells herself that her indiscretion doesn't count because it doesn't mean anything. Yet if both parties were to discover the whole truth about their partner's actions, they would be equally horrified. As a woman, Leila places far more importance on emotional intimacy than Jack. Her boyfriend confiding in and connecting with another woman, particularly when she feels so distant from him, seems like the ultimate insult. As a man, Jack is unlikely to appreciate the impact of his intimate dinners, but he would be furious to learn of Leila's seasonal smooching, because, as stated, men attach far more importance to physical connections.

Of course, the fact that men and women classify and approach infidelity so differently makes it all the more difficult to recover from the hurt. When he says, "But it was just a walk in the park!" she hears "I can't find the time or the energy to spend with you or invest in our emotional connection, but I feel so close to this other woman that I love spending quality time alone with her," even if he literally means "But it was just a walk in the park!" Likewise, when she comes home from work and says, "I love this new guy in Human Resources. He is so funny and literally has the whole office in stitches," he might well hear "This new guy is so popular and amusing. I love being around him. He's such an impressive man, so much better than you!" These misunderstandings occur every day, and to work through them, you need to learn to accept that the way you interpret a situation is not always the most accurate way. More often than not, you will see the situation through a filter created by your own viewpoint. Always make sure to ask yourself if what you are hearing is what he is saying. The more you can listen without coloring the situation, the better you can communicate with your partner and make him understand your point of view.

HOW TO MOVE FORWARD

Which way do we go after an infidelity? Do we subscribe to the "leopards can't change their spots" school of thought and kick our relationship to the curb? Or do we fall in with the "everyone deserves a second chance" crew and at least try to forgive and forget? Discussions about cheating and infidelity will always provoke a range of responses and opinions. We all have a friend who operates on a "one strike and you're out" basis, the hard, strong woman who won't stand for her partner so much as thinking about cheating before she's out the door. On the other end of the spectrum, we all know a long-suffering pal who relentlessly endures a serial cheater. The fact is, we all have different views on infidelity. Some people will always believe cheating is an inherently unforgivable sin. Others will always place faith in rehabilitation, claiming that unfaithfulness can occasionally be nothing more than a colossally senseless mistake and a relationship can survive if both parties are motivated to get through it.

And in a sense, both theories are right. Yet neither of them really matters. After you have been cheated on, once the dust settles and you've heard heated advice from your hairdresser, your best friend, and your aunt's neighbor's dog walker, in the end the only opinion that counts is yours. Moving on from infidelity is about establishing what you can live with. What will make you happy? How should you continue on, in the relationship or on your own? And the answer for most people is simple. To move on, we need to close chapters, we need to put a lid on things, we need to build a bridge over the past.

In a word, we need closure.

Think about it like a sumptuous seven-course meal in a fine-dining restaurant. Before moving on to the next course, a refreshing sorbet is offered to cleanse the palate, remove the taste of the previous dish, and prepare the taste buds for the next course. In order to really enjoy the next course, we close the door on the last dish. If you go hurtling from romantic episode to romantic episode without cleansing the traces of the last experience, you won't be able to truly enjoy what comes next; you will still carry the previous taste in your mouth. That might mean leaving your partner to his duck à l'orange while you grab a Big Mac elsewhere, or it might mean you cleanse together and settle down for the next course as a couple.

If you decide the relationship is worth salvaging, there has to be a way that both partners can accept, forgive, and move on. Closure comes from knowing that as a couple you have confronted the affair, surveyed the damage, dealt with the trauma, and learned to trust again. This can and probably will be a long and arduous process. Trust is a valuable commodity and it takes time to rebuild. Whatever the nature of the infidelity, from a one-night stand to a long-term affair, it is important that you and your partner address the threat posed to the relationship. Be honest about how it has affected the element of trust between you. Acknowledge that this element will take time to replenish and that it needs nurture and effort from both of you.

If you decide that you want your relationship to continue, then you need to face up to the real underlying issues behind the infidelity and find ways to move forward. You can do this by dealing with what happened. There are steps you can take to invest in the restructuring and rebuilding of your relationship:

Step #1: Acknowledge what happened and own your share of responsibility

Sounds obvious, right? Ever since we were at school we've been taught to own our actions and acknowledge when they are wrong. But it's remarkable how an infidelity can find us running scared from conceding our part in the drama. If you were unfaithful to your partner, you probably lied at some point, you definitely acted dishonorably, and you may have blatantly disregarded and disrespected your partner. The only way to move on from these hard, cold facts is to accept them. Admit to yourself and to your partner that you violated the relationship in these ways.

There's nothing harder than trying to forgive somebody who won't fully accept his or her guilt. Likewise, if you and your partner have been arguing for months, and the steady decline of the relationship led to an infidelity, then you probably need to assess your own behavior. Nobody's suggesting that a few spats justify a betrayal, but accepting your own involvement in the situation can help you understand it. Perhaps your partner felt shut out or isolated by you. This doesn't mean he has a right to cheat, but it may have implications for the way your relationship recovers and renews itself. Recognize this, accept your role in the proceedings, and be honest with yourself and with your partner.

Now, after both parties have assessed their behavior realistically, a plan of action will become clearer. It is easier to see the possible changes that will occur and to examine how these changes will affect the relationship. However disappointing or discouraging this might be, it is a more realistic and balanced way to look at things, at least until you have had time to begin rebuilding these crucial relationship components.

Step #2: Make a decision about what you can live with

We've touched on this. Nobody knows you better than yourself. And after spending twenty, thirty, forty years inside your body with your own set of tendencies and emotions, you should have a pretty good idea of what you can and can't tolerate within a relationship. You probably know what your own personal boundaries look like. It's easy to say "I forgive you," but saying it is about as effective as saying "You are healed" to a five-year-old with a bloody knee. The words mean nothing unless you've cleansed the wound, dealt with the pain, and sealed it off. If you know in your heart of hearts you will never be happy with somebody who was unfaithful to you, if you know deep down you will never forget, then you need to move on.

Whatever the wrongs or rights of the situation, you and your partner both deserve the best chance for happiness, and if that can't be achieved through pursuing your relationship, so be it. Don't beat a dead horse. If you know you will never recover from the infidelity, get out. And get out now, before you replace optimism with cynicism and start despising weddings, spitting at happy couples in the street, and booing Celine Dion's rendition of "The Power of Love."

It doesn't have to be the end, though. If you searched

your soul and decided that you *can* move on from this and you want your relationship to work, then that's great. Often, it's well worth a shot. Many couples come to counseling after infidelity has been discovered to make sure they are both equipped for the long haul. Each partner needs to think about whether it is possible to rebuild the trust in their relationship and then make a well-considered decision about the viability of the partnership.

Step #3: Rebuild trust and commitment

Making the decision to hit the road or stand by your man is the (relatively) easy part. After that comes the real hard work. If you decide that you want to salvage something from the infidelity wreckage and rebuild your relationship, then you need to accept that you have a long, occasionally painful, and often frustrating task ahead of you. The words "Let's move on" won't move your relationship back to full fruitful health. Nope. Both partners need to devote themselves to the process of rebuilding trust and commitment, and it will take a while.

You need to work on developing reasonable assumptions and expectations. What can really help is forming new ideas and boundaries about each other. More specifically, the newly shaped negative set of expectations each partner has of each other needs to be addressed and, where possible, challenged, in order for everyone to gain closure and regain emotional intimacy and trust. Beliefs such as "He is self-centered and only thinks about what he wants" or "She isn't the caring person I thought she was" will only destroy a relationship if they are allowed to fester. One of the first corrective steps is to reframe the betrayed mate's perspective of the offending partner. A good question to ask yourself, to challenge the belief that the infidelity is the end of your relationship, is "Is the offense really unforgivable?" As you try to reason and understand the circumstances which caused your partner to cross the line of fidelity, this question can provide some new meanings. Don't accept your deepest fears as gospel. Ask yourself how realistic they are. Does your partner drunkenly kissing some girl at his office party mean he thinks you're fat, hideous, and unlovable? No. It probably means he was drunk, foolish, and inconsiderate and is not a realistic indication of the way he views you. Challenge your thoughts, ask yourself if the infidelity renders your relationship irreparable, and be prepared to do some honest soul-searching.

To truly rebuild, you need to develop honest and open communication. Some basic rules for breaking old patterns of miscommunication include not blaming each other for whatever is wrong, speaking effectively about your thoughts and feelings, and listening to your partner. You're not communicating with your partner unless you're listening to him and trying to appreciate what he tells you. Even when it's painful, try to discuss issues. Avoiding conflict is not healthy, and trying to keep the peace will never be as powerful as speaking up. If it helps, use humor. Learning to laugh at the often absurd drama of the situation can help you vent your frustrations and remind you of the common ground you share.

Rebuilding trust can only happen when you focus on the realities rather than the illusions or false fantasies of the relationship. And it won't be an overnight miracle. Don't be scared of disrupting the peace once you and your partner have started to move through the trauma of infidelity.

It's far better to voice your concerns as they occur, rather than gradually building up a big knot of worry that's impossible to untangle once you decide to address it. If you feel untrusting or suspicious or insecure about the strength of your partner's commitment after an infidelity, express those emotions. Then you can confront them, examine them, and work toward a happier future for you both.

In all its forms, from a fumble on the photocopier at a Christmas party to a carefully executed full-blown affair, infidelity is always a tricky issue to navigate. It can shake your relationship to its foundation and have disastrous implications for the emotional well-being of everyone involved. And the scary thing is that an affair occurs in almost half of all relationships. But it does NOT have to mean the end.

Let's look at Joanne and Tim. They've been going out for five years but have experienced real problems within the last two. Joanne discovered that Tim slept with a work colleague, Lisa. They decided to work through things and put the infidelity behind them. Six months on, Tim casually mentions that he and Lisa met for dinner because she was feeling down about her mother's illness and needed someone to talk to.

> JOANNE: How could you do this to me? After all we've been though!

Joanne meant *I thought this was just about sex. I thought it was a stupid one-night stand that was over . . . now it's starting all over again!*

> TIM: (*Why is she so mad? I haven't done anything wrong here. It's not like I slept with her again.*) I

didn't do anything. She just needed someone to talk to.

Joanne heard *I am this woman's emotional support. She relies on me and opens up to me. Not like you.*

> JOANNE: This is worse than sleeping with her, Tim.
>
> TIM: (*She is being ridiculous.*) You're being unreasonable. You're determined to blame me for everything. Talking isn't cheating.
>
> JOANNE: (*By being an emotional support to this woman, you are betraying me. You don't love me enough to make this work.*)
>
> TIM: (*I can't do anything right. This is never going to work.*)

Regardless of who is the victim or the instigator of the affair, don't expect your partner to see things in exactly the same way you do. Tim and Joanne need to accept that a lack of consistency between their approaches to dealing with the affair doesn't always represent a lack of understanding or mean that their love is doomed to failure. You can work through this kind of problem by realizing that you experience it differently because you are a woman, and vice versa. Take time to understand his viewpoint, and take biological and societal factors into consideration. Understand the impact being a man will have on his behavior and factor that into your communication with him.

Finally, if you decide that you can't live with the pain of

the betrayal and that in order for you to move on, you actually need to leave the relationship, then leave. But don't let
the infidelity define you. Don't internalize the affair. While
it may be a reflection of your relationship, it probably isn't
a direct reflection on you. Infidelity is painful, heartbreaking, and potentially life changing, but it isn't the end of the
world. Not only can you recover from an affair, you can actually gain from one. Any painful experience gives us a chance
to learn about ourselves and a whole load of other useful
stuff like love, life, and relationships. Whatever your decision, take what you can from the incident, address it, and
then move on. Know yourself, know what you can tolerate,
and make sure that you ensure that your own emotional
well-being is foremost in your mind. And if that means
smashing up Celine Dion records, so be it.

TIPS TO REMEMBER

- Men and women often see sex very differently. A physical encounter might mean nothing to you but the
world to him.
- He won't see emotional connections in the way that
you do. A friendly chat with a woman may be just that
to him.
- Be honest about what you can get over and what you
can't.

CHAPTER 11

We Need to Talk

Jim and Sally have dated for three years. They started out like gangbusters, and the relationship quickly evolved. A year in, they were living together. But slowly over the past year, things have gone stale and they are not the same fun-loving couple. Arguments are the norm, and that first year is a distant memory.

> SALLY: I think we need to talk, Jim. We're just not getting along at the moment. It's argument after argument. What's wrong with us?

> JIM: What do you mean? I thought we were fine. Do you want to break up? Is that what you're trying to say?

> SALLY: No! It's just . . . we need to look at what's changed and why.

JIM: Let's just end it. If you're so unhappy with me, there's no point forcing it.

SALLY: That's not what I'm saying. Don't get so angry. I'd like to try to fix things and save this.

JIM: "Save this"? I had no idea we needed saving. Maybe we *should* break up.

Whether a relationship has been going for two months or two decades, the "We need to talk" moment is always difficult. Going through a tough patch that may lead to a breakup can leave a couple prone to misconceptions and miscommunications.

In the opening example, Sally is concerned about the relationship and tries to voice this to Jim. He takes it as a sign to break up, perhaps because he is afraid of being hurt and wants to end it first, to protect himself, or perhaps because he actually thinks things are over and is using this as his cue to finish it. One thing's for sure: The only way they can figure out what's really going on and whether they should stay and fight for their relationship or call it a day is by learning to better communicate how they're really feeling. This becomes very difficult when you throw painful feelings into the mix.

The thing is, when we enter into a relationship with someone, we make certain emotional investments. We make sacrifices and adapt our lives to accommodate our fantastic new partner. If everything goes wrong, the transition from being that person's "one" to possibly becoming their ex can be a tough one to work through.

Deciding whether or not to break up a relationship is never simple. Men and women view the reasons for a relationship going wrong very differently. One study conducted by researchers at Francis Marion University found that when men initiated a breakup, they saw it as a joint decision, but when they were the dumpees, they saw it as the sole responsibility of their partner. Women did not see the situation in such a biased way and were more likely to think both were to blame, whether they did the dumping or were dumped. When men initiated the breakup, they saw the relationship as completely over, but when they were the ones broken up with, they weren't so final about things. Also, when men were dumped, they described their partner's actions as manipulative. Overall, the researchers found that, perhaps surprisingly, men are more distressed by a relationship going wrong than women and are more likely to try to rekindle the old relationship.

Clearly these results fly in the face of the assumption that women invest more into relationships than men, at least on an emotional level. More importantly, it highlights how perceptions are colored by gender tendencies.

Regardless of gender, the breakdown of a relationship is tough. From the first time you get shunned on the school playground to the endless hours of your adult life you spend worrying about how to save your marriage, everyone who has been in a romantic relationship finds this to be true somewhere along the way. Relationships break down for all manner of reasons. Sometimes couples hurt each other to a point where repair is no longer possible. Sometimes people change and the relationship is not strong enough to adapt. Sometimes people suddenly confront underlying relationship or character flaws they always knew were there but chose to ignore. And sometimes, frustratingly, the relationship just isn't right anymore and both parties know they need to move on.

At best, this process is awkward; at worst, it is downright heartbreaking. But having a rough patch needn't spell the end for you and your man. Plenty of couples go through problems and come out again on the other side, often with renewed love and respect for each other. The trick is identifying the problem signs to watch out for, trying to fix them together, and, of course, knowing when to leave if that is the best option.

SPOTTING THE WARNING SIGNS

When it comes to problems in a relationship, a man will usually prefer to withdraw and think, whereas a woman will want to talk about it. In the man's eyes, once a problem has been aired, the onus is on finding a solution and getting on with it. Conversely, nothing appeals more to a stressed-out female than the chance to dissect, analyze, and relive every moment of the disagreement or problem.

These differences dramatically affect how the two genders react during a relationship crisis. Women are more likely than men to become demanding and will push for issues to be addressed. However, this doesn't sit particularly well with a man's tendency to sit back and avoid confrontation on relationship issues. His reluctance to talk will often be interpreted as a lack of concern or effort. Equally, a man is likely to become increasingly irritated by the female push to discuss, discuss, discuss and will actually retreat further from the relationship.

Take a look at Debbie and Jason. They have been going out for six years now and recently it feels like there's a brick wall between them. They don't make each other laugh, they don't connect with each other, and they don't share anything anymore. Debbie tries to raise the issue with Jason after one particularly awkward night.

> DEBBIE: What's wrong with you? We need to talk!

Jason heard *You're making me unhappy! Explain yourself!*

> JASON: (*This is a two-way street and I'm not massively happy either, but what difference will talking make?*) Nothing's wrong. I'm fine.

Debbie heard *I can't be bothered to discuss this.*

> DEBBIE: (*The only way to sort this out is to discuss it. He obviously doesn't care enough to want to sort things out.*) If you loved me you'd be honest with me.

> JASON: (*Don't blackmail me.*) I'm going out.

While a man's solution will be to carry on with life regardless, a woman's will usually be to dissect, discuss, and analyze. Both sides will act according to their specific stereo-type and not get the results they need. Each partner must learn how to raise the topic in a way that allows both sides to feel comfortable.

HOW TO BROACH THE SUBJECT

There are few things worse than the daily drudgery of endur-ing a relationship that has lost its spark. Nobody wants to stick with a situation that's making them unhappy, but com-municating these desperate feelings to a partner can feel like mission impossible.

The key thing here is to remember that your perception of the situation will undoubtedly be colored by your own emotions and beliefs. It rarely occurs to us that our negative judgments could be wrong and that when we criticize our partner or the relationship, we are actually attacking a dis-torted image. All too often we behave in a way that invites or even ensures a predictable response, thus confirming a core belief we have. For example, if we feel unloved, these nega-tive thoughts lead us to behave in an irritable manner, which in turn provokes a fight with our partner. We then interpret their behavior as evidence to support our original theory.

Avoid jumping to conclusions about your partner's behav-ior. Instead, try to take a step back from the situation and establish an objective viewpoint. And when your partner tries to communicate, listen to what he is actually saying, not what you assume he is saying. Remember that you will never know what your partner is trying to say better than he does, so listen properly—not through a filter that blocks out any words that may disprove your long-established assumptions.

At this stage it's important to nip negativity in the bud, since once it begins it can become all-encompassing and self-fulfilling. The more negatively we feel about a situation, the more prone we are to noticing everything that's imperfect. For example, if we are sick of what we interpret as a constant stream of selfish behavior from our partner, we are more likely to notice that, once again, he left the toilet seat up and see it as a sign that he doesn't care enough about us or the relationship. Imagine the difference between these two scenarios. The first is Veronica and Mark, two months into their relationship.

> VERONICA: Are you hungry? I made lasagna.
>
> MARK: I'm good, thanks. I had a big lunch. I was actually thinking we could go over to my mom's tonight. What do you say?
>
> VERONICA: Sure, I can always stick this in the freezer. I'll jump in the shower and be ready in ten.

Now imagine the same scenario after two years and a period of conflict:

> VERONICA: Are you hungry? I made lasagna.
>
> MARK: I'm good. I had a big lunch. I'm heading over to my mom's tonight if you want to come.

VERONICA: Oh, I see. You waltz in, turn your nose up at my cooking, and then assume I want to just go along with your plans and undoubtedly watch you dive into a four-course meal at your mother's.

The situation hasn't changed, but the general state of the relationship has. The personalities haven't changed, but the way actions and words are interpreted has.

Negativity within our own relationship can actually alter the way we see the wider world. In its simplest sense, perhaps, this can explain the difference between seeing a romantic film and weeping tears of real emotion or making exaggerated vomiting sounds and shooting cynical looks at the screen. When we feel negatively about our love, we feel negatively about love in general. When we don't feel too great about our world, we don't feel too great about anything in the universe. When discussing relationship issues with your partner, bear this in mind and try to prevent general feelings of negativity from coloring your success moving forward.

This is easier said than done. The problem is that you never see the negativity coming; you can't plan for it. Back in the "No you hang up, no you hang up" days when every moment together felt like a blessing, you never anticipated the days when your relationship actually makes you feel worse about yourself and the world, not better. You're never prepared for the moment you realize that everything your boyfriend does annoys you. And you never want to deal with the disastrous realization when the thought of seeing your man turns from an in-stomach butterfly explosion to a sinking slump. As things get worse, optimism is the first casualty. The arguments continue, and it can feel like you are on a one-way path to the messiest breakup of all time. But this doesn't have to be your only option.

Developing the communication tools to empower you and your partner to look at issues objectively is necessary when your relationship hits the "We need to talk" stage. You need to establish the right solution for both of you, whether that means working at your relationship or kissing it goodbye. Navigating this huge decision with your partner can be tricky, but there are some tips to help ease the journey. These are great things to implement whenever you are fighting (fair), but are crucial to keep in mind during the critical "We need to talk" stage of any relationship.

Tip #1: Be willing to compromise and see things from another perspective

No one can save a relationship by herself. Putting your relationship back on track requires effort and effective communication in abundance from both partners. You need to think in terms of cooperation rather than confrontation.

In order to strive for a more balanced view, you both need to try to concentrate on your partner's strengths and reflect on your own contribution to the problems. How one partner perceives and interprets what the other does is far more important in determining satisfaction in the relationship than the actions themselves. In other words, it usually isn't what your partner actually does that is the problem, it's the way you interpret it.

If you and your partner both want to save your relationship, you both have to be prepared to distance yourselves from your own interpretations of events and accept that your view of things is not necessarily 100 percent correct. If you can't start with a willingness to compromise and discuss without prejudice, it's unlikely that your attempts at reconciliation will ever get off the ground. Remember, it takes two, baby!

Tip #2: Know what you want and be assertive
Many couples remain stuck in a rut because they shy away from articulating what it is they really want. This might be through fear of their partner's response. We might feel that self-sacrifice is preferable to the risk of causing pain or anger to the ones we love. We hold our own wants and needs inside, preferring to attend to those of our partner. In the long run, this will only contribute to feelings of resentment and negativity.

Problems can also arise when people swing between passive and aggressive styles and find it hard to strike a balance. Let's look at Kelly and Bill. Deep down, Kelly is scared that her dreams for the relationship are different from Bill's. Rather than express what she actually wants, she devotes her efforts to meeting Bill's expectations. This is exhausting and unfulfilling, and after a few months, she tires of the continual attempts to please. She then shifts the balance by making unreasonable demands on Bill and expecting him to emulate her previous submissive behavior. The end result, particularly for Bill, is a big confusing mess.

Genuinely asserting yourself is not about reacting irrationally to a long-established situation like the one described above. It's an ability to communicate your needs, wants, and feelings clearly and confidently while at the same time respecting those of your partner. Being assertive encourages positive emotions and prevents painful emotions like anger, hurt, frustration, and disappointment from developing in the first place. The more assertive a person becomes, the more comfortable she will feel in any situation. Assertiveness in relationships is all about honest, open communication and compromise where both parties feel understood and heard.

Another important aspect of being assertive is the ability to say no to requests. For some people this is especially difficult as they see it as upsetting or disappointing. However, saying no means that, without being selfish, you set limits on other people's requests for your time and energy if they conflict with your own needs and desires.

If your partner invites some friends to spend the evening and you return home from a hellish day at work, there's no shame saying, "I understand you would like to spend the evening with your friends, but I have had a really long day and feel exhausted. I need to pass on tonight. Would there be another night when we could all get together?" Being assertive doesn't mean being confrontational; it means having the self-respect and self-care skills to acknowledge and address your own needs.

Tip #3: Cope with criticism
The crucial element of every disagreement is the difference in the way partners view the same event. Partners quite often perceive each other's questions, requests, or statements as blaming or attacking. Criticism can take on a life of

its own when a couple is hammering out what is wrong with their relationship. You need to stay above the drama, so you can view the situation calmly and accurately.

Judith and Brett have been married for five years now. They met through friends, and they couldn't believe their luck. They were perfect for each other. He loved the left side of the bed; she just had to sleep on the right. He loved dogs; she hated cats. You get the picture. However, things have stalled lately, and they are experiencing major communication problems. Here's a typical exchange after a heated fight over his friendship with an ex-girlfriend:

JUDITH: Let's talk about what happened.

BRETT: (*What's the point? We will just go around in circles.*) Not now, it's not a good time.

JUDITH: (*This is serious. Why won't he work through it with me?*) What's wrong with you?

BRETT: (*Everything always has to be on her terms. I don't want to talk about this now.*) Not now!

JUDITH: (*How dare you talk to me like a child.*) I have had enough of this!

When someone feels she is being criticized by her partner, there are two common reactions. The first is to crumble and feel rejected. The second is to defend herself from criticism by becoming critical herself. Criticism is perceived as a direct threat to self-esteem.

The real skill here is learning how to pass comment on

negative elements of your relationship without resorting to blame and put-downs. If you can both master this, it means you have two new choices. Now, upon receiving criticism, you can stand your ground and assert your own opinion confidently, but without trying to score a point off of your partner. Or you can accept that the criticism might just be fair and look at how you can work on this aspect of your behavior.

Keep in mind that the difference between "You make me feel insecure when you do that" and "I feel insecure when this happens" is monumental. One statement is accusing and attributes the negative emotions to your partner. The other statement accepts that your feelings are your own responsibility while still asserting you are unhappy with the situation. If you get into the habit of using "I," it can magically transform communication with your partner!

Tip # 4: Learn to cope with anger

It is normal to feel angry sometimes. However, anger is often problematic for many people. Sometimes the problems arise from an inability to control anger. For others, the problems lie in a tendency to ignore anything unpleasant for fear of provoking anger or bad feelings. The bottom line is we get most angry with those we are in close relationships with because we expect the most from them.

The emotion of anger can range from irritation to rage. How angry we become in a given situation is influenced by our interpretation of the meaning of that event. It might seem ridiculous how often we blame our negative emotions on other people's behavior, but actually nobody else can single-handedly cause you to feel angry, resentful, or frustrated.

Other people may say or do all kinds of things, but it is your interpretation of their behavior that makes you mad. *Assertive* people will let the other person know that their actions at that particular time are very annoying but they are willing to take ultimate responsibility for the feelings that pop up. They can express their anger without being demeaning or unloving. In contrast, *aggressive* behavior threatens a person and makes it difficult to connect with what they are trying to convey.

You need to remember that anger is best expressed as soon as you feel it. When things are left unsaid, the feeling continues to exist under the surface. When it finally comes out it becomes aggression, sarcasm, or bitterness. Let your man know how you feel, briefly and simply. It is better to say less than more.

Tip #5: If all else fails, consider a trial separation
A trial separation can bridge the gap between being together and being apart. Often, this will give you the time to reflect, consider how your differences may be coloring your views, and work out what is really right for you. It might mean that you and your partner end things, but equally it might give new insight into ways you can restructure your relationship to ensure success as you move forward.

SHOULD I STAY OR SHOULD I GO?

Trying to fix a relationship is tough. What he sees as manipulation, you see as careful contemplation. What he sees as the end of the road, you see as a short break. Men and women will approach, negotiate, and reflect on a problem completely differently, and this can make the process a million times more complicated.

But now, after you feel like you've tried everything and nothing has worked, you're still not sure whether to throw in the towel. Should you and your partner part ways or stick with it? A good rule of thumb here is to plot your relationship on an imaginary pie chart displaying happiness and unhappiness. If the amount of time you are unhappy because of your relationship greatly overshadows the amount of time you are happy because of it, it's probably time to move on. After all, the point of a relationship is to enhance your life, and if it has stopped doing this, it's very hard to justify investing the necessary time and effort required to keep it going. Be prepared to admit that this isn't necessarily your partner's fault or the sign of an awful relationship doomed from the start. It may just boil down to a basic flaw in communications. Your inability to tackle this as a couple is likely to be due to you as much as it is to your partner.

If you still decide to stick with it, remember that you can't do it by yourself. A relationship comprises two human beings. For it to flourish and survive, it must be nurtured, supported, and strengthened by both. If your partner can't dedicate himself to the cause in the same way you can, you're probably fighting an impossible battle. Whatever your decision, open, assertive communication is vital. Focus on respect and negotiation rather than blame and resentment.

Of course, as anyone who's attempted to navigate a "bad patch" or "the end of the road" knows, this doesn't mean you and your partner will necessarily hit the mutual satisfaction part of the plan. If you can, that's great. But if you can't, then it may well be time to close the door on your time together.

Yes, be angry. Yes, be sad. But try to express these emotions in a way that won't provoke your partner, or indeed, prolong the inevitable. Don't let "I can't believe it's over" turn into "You've ruined the relationship." Don't let "I'm so angry that we can't talk to each other like we used to" become "You selfish, uptight idiot." If you and your partner can develop the communication tools to express your feelings in a nonaggressive, neutral way, the process will be easier and less stressful and will result in far fewer smashed hopes, dreams, and photo frames.

TIPS TO REMEMBER

- Even if you want to talk things through, accept that your partner might not at first. It's not him being awkward; it's how he's built psychologically. Try to find a common ground that feels comfortable for both of you.
- Learn how to link what you think you need with what you are saying. Work out what will make you happy and find a way to explain it that makes sense to your partner.
- Don't play games. Be honest. If you are sad or angry or jealous, then be open. Holding back will only cause you to build resentment.
- Don't always see a relationship breakdown as a terrible thing. Sometimes it can open the door to a far more productive and healthy stage in your life.

Marriage Material

Jeff and Sonia started dating three years ago and have lived together for over year. Everything is going great. They enjoy their time together, but Sonia is wondering when he'll pop the question.

> JEFF: I just don't understand why you're so obsessed with the whole "marriage" thing. You always say we have the perfect relationship.
>
> SONIA: I want the relationship to progress.
>
> JEFF: You mean you want children?
>
> SONIA: No, I mean I want some security. I want to know we're committed, that this is forever.
>
> JEFF: Okay, well, I *am* committed, this *is* forever. Jeez, we own a house together. What more security do you want?

SONIA: I want to get married. Why can't you understand that?

Indeed. Why can't Jeff understand Sonia's need to have a
ring on her finger, a certificate, and the official stamp of coupledom? Well, it's not just Jeff. It's the same with many men.
Although men who come from traditional backgrounds are
more likely to embrace the tradition of marriage and have
positive feelings about marriage, there is a core of men resolutely opposed to the very idea. And these men aren't just
against tying the knot. They are less likely to believe a partner is telling the truth about previous relationships, more
likely to dread divorce, and more likely to say that single
men have better sex lives than married men. Many of them
see marriage as losing their personal freedom.

Interestingly it's not just young twenty-something guys
who are afraid to settle down, but those well into their
thirties. Clearly this flies in the face of reason when you
consider research that consistently shows that married men
live longer and are healthier and happier than their single
counterparts. Surely in this age of sexual equality and female
liberation men can't really view marriage as a lifetime of cur-
tailed fun and misery. Is marriage really still such a big deal,
such a scary proposition?

It seems so. Making the transition from boyfriend and
girlfriend to man and wife is a huge step for any relationship.
We are talking about a lifelong commitment. Like it or not,
marriage still constitutes one of the most celebrated and
widely recognized rituals in modern society. It means that
you suddenly have to tick different boxes on all those forms
you fill in. And it means that you make a solemn promise to

share the good, the bad, and the ugly with another person for the rest of your life. No wonder men break out in a cold sweat at the mention of the "M" word.

Now, despite research on the reported reluctance of men to pick a ring and don a suit, figures show marriage to be more popular than ever. As society's standards of acceptability have shifted over the years, people are certainly in less of a rush to get married, but they definitely aren't abandoning the idea altogether.

The reasons for delaying marriage today tend to be educational and career aspirations. On average, men wait until they are thirty-one to say "I do," while women wait until they are twenty-six years old, according to the U.S. Census Bureau. The fact is that marriage is still seen as an aspiration, a goal, and a natural progression for most couples.

But that's not to say it isn't an institution that men and women view very differently. Marriage still represents a point of contention within many relationships and, as we've seen, particularly for some men. Some worry it will have detrimental effects on the relationship. After all, if everything seems to be going well, why risk ruining things with such a dramatic change? Other couples experience a huge imbalance in each partner's expectations of when, why, and how marriage should be considered, leading to loads of conflict.

WHY GET MARRIED?

Marriage is, for most, the ultimate intimate relationship in which we voluntarily enter. It's similar to the relationships we share with our parents and siblings in terms of the time spent together and bonds formed. And it's no wonder that so many people choose to make this commitment. Society sells marriage to us incredibly effectively. Marital relationships are portrayed in the media as sources of lifelong companionship, romance, support, sexual fulfillment, commitment, and individual well-being.

Being married can help protect individuals from life strains and provide a sense of security and purpose. Not only is marriage supposed to provide some semblance of a safety net between you and the big bad world as you and your partner help each other through difficult times, but it also performs a role in society. This is particularly relevant with regards to having and raising children. Marriage defines the legal responsibilities of each parent and also nails down the roles of each partner as mother and wife, father and husband. In this respect, marriage can be seen as a type of concrete that sets your relationship in stone and provides a universally recognized family structure.

ARE YOU READY FOR MARRIAGE?

The level of commitment, the amount of conflict, and the decisiveness of each partner are strong indicators of readiness for marriage. Interestingly, the course of a relationship is influenced more by male than by female desires and concerns. Basically, if the male asserts that he wants to get married, the couple is more likely to make it down the aisle than if the woman is the one who wants to tie the knot. Not really fair, is it?

What is certainly true is that the way men and women

view marriage is largely due to our firsthand experiences of witnessing the failures or successes of marriages around us. Obviously the most immediate and direct experience of marriage most of us witness is that of our parents. Just as if we are taught to enjoy reading from an early age as a child we are more likely to turn into good spellers, if we observe and learn from a good marriage we are more likely to go on to form our own good marriage. Our feelings about marriage are likely to be more positive, and consequently we will be more relaxed, less anxious about it.

Roy and Marisa have dated for four years. They are both in their early thirties. Roy is absolutely certain Marisa is the one he wants to marry, and he has made this clear to her many times. However, Marisa grew up in a household barely held together by two adults who essentially hated each other. Her father was controlling, her mother weak. When they finally divorced, once Marissa had grown up and moved out, both denounced the partnership as the worst mistake of their lives. Now, years later, her parents are still bitter and unable to move on. Marissa is very happy with Roy, but her firsthand experience causes her to view marriage negatively. Roy doesn't understand her reluctance because his parents have been happily married for forty years. Their differing viewpoints will color their discussions on the subject.

ROY: I can't wait for the day we walk down the aisle.

Roy meant *I love you and wish you would be a little more open-minded about this.*

Marisa heard *You're not committed to this relationship!*

Our relationship will only feel complete once we are married.

> MARISA: (*Why won't you drop this? I love you but marriage will only end in heartbreak.*) That would be great. We can spend the next forty years of our lives making each other miserable?

Roy heard *I don't want to make that kind of commitment to you. Marrying you would be a disaster.*

These differences highlight the need for open communication. You both need to appreciate that the decision to marry isn't as simple as "I love you" or "I don't love you." A whole host of factors come into play. Recognizing the role that your upbringing and the events in your life play in your readiness for marriage is really important. And all this before you've even begun to look at the issues that arise just because he is a man and you are a woman.

A TALE OF TWO GENDERS

The story of any married couple is always the tale of two people. Although they may experience the same events, the reality for each partner will be different. And these differences are likely to be partly a result of our gender-specific traits and emotional tendencies, as well as a result of the expectations that society places on us based purely on whether we are male or female. Marriage is a highly gendered institution. To a certain extent, men are still expected to be the breadwinner and anchor of the family in the outside world. Meanwhile, women are expected to adopt a more expressive role as a homemaker, even if she has her own outside career, and the anchor of the family internally. This stereotype explains why successful women are far less likely to marry than their male counterparts.

When men remain single, it is seen as a choice or even a lucky escape from marriage as they revel in the freedom and fun of the single life, while single women are seen in a relentless search for some hapless schlub to tie down. This is rarely true, and in fact research shows that healthy, emotionally sound women actually often take longer to commit and settle down than other women. But the stereotype remains. Hence women are pressured to care more about marriage, and as a result, they usually end up investing more into the idea than men. Of course these stereotypes don't apply to every couple. They probably apply to fewer couples in today's world of increasing sexual equality. But they can go some way to explaining why couples see marriage so differently.

Tom and Angie are both in their early thirties. After living together for five years, they both struggle with deciding on the next step. Angie wants to get married and has made this blatantly clear to Tom, who feels exactly the opposite. As far as Tom is concerned, marriage is an unnecessary formality that exists to make others happy. He doesn't want to march down the aisle just so that Angie's mom can have a chance to get her wedding hat out of the closet. For him marriage is about fulfilling the expectations of others, and he considers himself perfectly happy within his existing relationship with Angie. However, this isn't being communicated successfully to Angie. She interprets his reluctance to pop the question as a sign he doesn't love her enough and doesn't picture her in his future. When Angie says, "It would be so cool to call you my husband!" Tom hears "Everyone else is getting married! Why can't we?!" Likewise, when Tom says, "Spending tens of thousands of dollars on a big party and a piece of paper seems like a waste of money," Angie hears "I'm not spending that money on you because I don't want to commit to you. Someone better might come along next week." To untangle this "He says, she hears" mess is to establish the reality behind each partner's words.

Angie needs to articulate her real motivations behind wanting to get married: to demonstrate her commitment to him, to provide a traditional home for their future children, and to show how proud she is of him that she wants to be recognized as "his" in the most official way possible. Tom's defenses will likely relax. Equally, Tom must explain that although he feels strongly about Angie and wants to make a commitment too, he doesn't need a big ceremony to prove it and doesn't feel comfortable making such an exhibition. Angie will then feel secure and better prepared to negotiate. Once Angie and Tom begin to deal in truths rather than assumptions, they are halfway to establishing a compromise.

MARRIAGE—THE VITAL INGREDIENTS

You and your partner love each other. You know that you care about each other's welfare, you want to make each other happy, and you still get that little weird butterfly thing in your stomach when he calls. But is that enough to build a marriage? Quite frankly, no. Because while love and genuine affection provide you with the incentive needed to overcome differences and work through problems, they aren't enough on their own. It takes much more for a marriage to really work.

There are several factors that ensure a successful marriage. And they are particularly useful yardsticks if you are deciding whether or not you are ready to walk down the aisle. As you read through each of the points below, decide how closely they reflect your relationship and compare that with the way your partner deals with and feels about these factors. This activity can be really helpful, not because you have to abandon the relationship if you don't agree on everything, but because it can help you identify areas you can work on to make things better.

Commitment

What It Means
Are you in the marriage for the long haul, whatever happens and whatever issues you have to face as a couple? Are you both prepared to assume responsibility for each other's happiness, come what may, through thick and thin? Commitment means reliability and a sense of security for both partners. To achieve it, we need to know what to expect from our partner and that we can rely on him.

What to Watch Out For
Problems with commitment can manifest themselves in a number of ways: your partner being overcritical of your flaws,

expressing fear of being permanently trapped, looking for an "out" to the relationship, or avoiding emotional intimacy and affection. People tend to act like this when they hold fixed core beliefs such as "I cannot be dependent. I must not make myself vulnerable." And people who hold these beliefs are usually fearful that they will be hurt or rejected if they commit. But by trying to avoid being hurt, a vicious cycle of reinforcing that exact fear is set up as the person constantly enters unstable relationships that ultimately break up.

Ask yourself whether you and your man are equally committed to the relationship. If not, figure out why this might be and find ways you can express these concerns and address them together. A marriage will not flourish if one partner embarks upon it halfheartedly. Before you make the leap, you need to be sure that your partner is ready to commit himself fully in the same way that you are.

Loyalty and Trust

What It Means
When we talk about loyalty and trust, what we are talking about is the promise that you are both dedicated to each other's best interests and that neither of you will deliberately hurt the other. If trust is there, it allows couples to be at ease with each other, rather than constantly suspecting ulterior motives or bad intentions.

What to Watch Out For

The opposite of trust occurs if your man is unable to make a total commitment or doesn't take responsibility for his actions. It might mean he's unwilling to make sacrifices, is looking for an escape route, or is even unfaithful. Again, you need to ask yourself whether your partner (or you) display this behavior. Just like commitment, trust and loyalty are reciprocal qualities, and they are only real if both partners feel them.

Cooperation

What It Means

Can you and your partner work together? Have you identified joint goals in life that you want to work toward achieving together? Are both of you happy to take responsibility for making decisions that will affect you as a pair? It relates to your willingness to deal with conflicts and difficult situations. If you can cooperate together, these issues can be accepted and resolved.

What to Watch Out For

Where there is a lack of cooperation within a relationship, it's often because one partner is behaving in a self-centered way. It may be that your partner ignores your decisions and wishes, to the point of being deceitful. Think hard about this one. Do you and your partner have shared goals? Does he want the same things you want for yourself? Do you both want the same things in terms of where you live, whether you have children, and how many? Couples who share goals and work together to achieve them have a far greater chance of going the distance.

HOW DO YOU KNOW YOU'RE READY TO TAKE THE PLUNGE?

Clearly, it's vital that both of your views on the meaning of getting married are similar. Failure to appreciate differences can make the transition extremely difficult. This often leads to getting stuck rather than getting married! Real communication becomes obscured by the need to enforce what you want. If you're desperate to get married and your partner isn't, you each become more fixed in your viewpoints. In this situation you both need to step back and reflect. The reluctant partner needs to think about exactly what it is he's fearful of, and ask himself honestly what is coloring his view. Perhaps his family experiences were bad or his parents were divorced and therefore he finds it hard to commit, or maybe his family has high expectations of a "perfect marriage." These issues should and can be addressed and resolved early on.

An important clue that you and your partner are ready to make the transition is the development of a "couple style," the way the two of you work together in a relationship, that is comfortable and works for both of you. The following questions will help you determine whether or not you and your partner have developed and settled into a "couple style" that can lend itself to a happy marriage:

Do you spend quality couple time together?

Remember those days when you and your partner actually *did* things? At the beginning of a relationship, the focus is usually on finding activities you both enjoy and using them to get to know each other. As the relationship solidifies and becomes more reliable, this quality time often gets neglected. After all, if you live together, you already spend enough time with each other, right? Wrong. There is a huge difference between sharing another TV dinner in silence and actually enjoying each other's company. Quality couple time means sharing activities. It means feeling close and nurturing your relationship. It could involve sharing concerns and feelings, discussing your dream house, or taking a few days off to do things together.

When we are ready to marry, the lure of the singles scene doesn't shine quite so brightly. Instead, we get more pleasure from time with our partner and appreciate the benefits of a trusting, committed relationship with one person as opposed to a schedule packed with different dates and parties.

How intimate are you?

In a happy, healthy relationship, emotional intimacy and sexual intimacy are very important. Emotional intimacy means that you and your partner know and understand each other's personalities and that you are aware of and sensitive to each other's hopes, dreams, and anxieties. You should be comfortable divulging inner thoughts to each other. Equally, sexual intimacy means you and your partner are happy and comfortable confiding your feelings about sex, your fantasies and your insecurities. A healthy sexual bond is crucial to a long and happy marriage and should never be underestimated in terms of importance. Do you and your partner feel entirely comfortable with each other? Are there things you don't feel that you can share with each other? A successful "couple style" will show emotional and physical intimacy or at least recognize how important they are and work toward achieving them.

Do you feel loved?

Loving someone is one thing. Feeling, indeed *knowing*, that they love you is just as important. When we feel loved and secure within a relationship, we are comfortable being ourselves and revealing the good, bad, and ugly aspects of our personalities. In a well-functioning couple, both partners embrace the fact that their other half knows them inside out and still loves them. This security allows us to be open, honest, and vulnerable.

Feeling loved is what will get you and your partner through the bad times. In the eye of the storm, knowing that your partner loves you unconditionally will protect you, strengthen you, and eventually carry you through.

Do you have positive expectations of marriage?

Remember the old adage "You reap what you sow"? Well, the more you put into your marriage, the more you stand to gain. If your husband-to-be trudges down the aisle, moaning about his loss of freedom and basically buying into the stereotype of men as commitment phobes who are restricted by marriage, it doesn't bode well. The decision to tie the knot should be a positive one that's shared by both partners. Be excited, be enthusiastic, and enjoy it.

Having said this, you should also be realistic. Before you trot into the church, you and your partner should face wedded life head-on. Recognize that hearts, flowers, and fantastic sex come as part of a package that also includes frustration, conflict, and compromise. That's not to say that your marriage won't be everything you dreamed it would be. It just means that you have to accept the rough with the smooth. Marriage is hard work, but as long as you accept this from the start you should have no problem addressing the challenges it throws at you.

Are you in his future plans?

Do you and your partner have the same dreams for the future? Do you trust each other to work at achieving and realizing these dreams? When you commit to a marriage, you commit to a shared future, so it's important that you establish whether you actually want the same things from life. Issues such as having children and where you live may be easy to ignore when you don't foresee them arising for another ten years, but it is impossible to build a happy, healthy marriage on false expectations.

Be honest, right from the start, about what you want from your marriage and encourage your partner to do the same. Then ensure that you are both committed to transforming these aspirations into a shared reality. The way your partner behaves should help you ascertain whether or not you can trust him to make this commitment. If either of you has a habit of talking the talk and then failing to walk the walk, the chances of you dedicating yourselves to these lifetime goals are slim. Be aware of this and work on it.

Making It Work

Gina and Max are both in their late twenties. Ever since Gina was little, she dreamed about being a bride and a wife. She and Max have been together for four years and both are absolutely convinced that they have found "the one." But while Gina is ready to stop dreaming about dresses and ready to start getting fitted, Max still sees himself as the independent guy he was ten years ago—albeit with a beautiful girlfriend he loves dearly.

Max knows Gina is ready to settle down, due to the endless bridal magazines left lying around and the surreptitious lingering by the jewelers' windows. But to Max, marriage means he must say good-bye to his youth. He's heard the tales about how women rule the roost once they wear a wedding band, and essentially, he's running scared. A person's self-concept, the way he sees and values himself, can take a bit of time to incorporate a new label such as "husband."

Of course, he's never actually asked Gina why she wants to get married. He assumes she does so she can chain him to the house, ban him from seeing his friends, and bombard him with forty years of chat about home furnishings, child-care theories, and dinner parties. When she says, "You'd look so gorgeous in a tuxedo," he hears "Get ready to mourn your freedom and your old life."

For Gina, the reality is rather different. She leads an active social life, and the last thing she wants is to tie Max down and restrict him. The problem is that she's struggling against twenty-six years of social conditioning that have taught Max to feel like marriage is a sacrifice rather than a positive choice. The words "husband" and "wife" are loaded with meaning, including a sense of serious responsibilities not imposed on those *just* living together.

The challenge is for Gina to spin marriage in a different way for Max. She needs to explain very clearly what marriage means to her and what it doesn't, so he can see the many positives that come from being man and wife. Max needs to articulate his fears and concerns about marriage so Gina can understand his reluctance and help allay these anxieties.

Right now, couples are freer than ever to dictate the path of their own relationship. Social expectations have relaxed, and consequently it's acceptable to try living together before marriage. But, with the guidelines blurred, marriage often becomes a breeding ground for conflict and misunderstanding.

As with all miscommunication, the answer in deciding whether to get married lies in battling through those gender-loaded conversations and working out what the real emotions behind the words are. Be honest with your partner, be genuine about your motivations, and be realistic about the best decision for your relationship. Work out if, deep down, you both want the same future, and you'll be on your way to determining whether this decision-making process ends in "I do," "I will . . . but not just yet," or "Not now or ever."

And keep in mind, marriage is not the end of the journey; it is the start of a new happy chapter in both of your lives. You need to continue applying everything you have learned about communicating and listening to your relationship.

Don't fall into the trap that once you have both said your vows, the work is done. The work is just beginning. The good news is, if you have really listened to each other and yourselves, you will have built a great foundation that will help you handle anything that married life throws your way.

TIPS TO REMEMBER

- Make your partner realize that you don't expect or want marriage to restrict his lifestyle or threaten his freedom.
- Don't assume your partner doesn't want to marry you for one reason or another. Talk to him. Establish his motivations.
- Don't see marriage as the ultimate goal. View it as a happy, healthy relationship whose objective is to make both of you feel loved and secure.
- Remember that "not yet" doesn't mean "I don't love you enough."

CHAPTER 13

A Real Life Happily Ever After

RAPUNZEL: Thank you, my handsome prince, for rescuing me. I'm so in love with you. Now what?

PRINCE CHARMING: Well, I figured I'd whisk you back to my castle and marry you.

RAPUNZEL: Sounds good to me. I was thinking that we should have a couple of children, as well.

PRINCE CHARMING: Lovely, we'll do that straight after a very glamorous wedding.

RAPUNZEL: Can't wait to meet the king and queen. Will we be living with them or will we have our own castle?

PRINCE CHARMING: We'll have our own castle, of course, but Mom and Dad will be right next door, for babysitting.

RAPUNZEL: Perfect. Hurrah, my life is all mapped out and I never need worry again.

We all know how the fairy tale ends. After the trials and tribulations, the wicked witches and poisoned apples, the beanstalks and ivory towers, the guy gets his girl and rides off with her into the sunset. They settle down, he trades the white horse for a nice fuel-efficient car, she cuts her long hair because while it's a godsend when you're stuck in a twenty-foot tower, it's a nightmare to style once you're back on level ground, and they take out a substantial mortgage on a three-bedroom colonial in the suburbs. And, of course, they live happily ever after.

Although the children's fairy tale is one of the first examples we are given of romantic relationships, the truth is that perfect couples don't exist, love needs to be worked on, and romantic relationships require time, patience, and regular maintenance. Before you run for the nunnery, these stark realities should not be seen as negatives. They are just facts of life. A romantic relationship features two personalities. This is what makes it so interesting, and, at the same time, what triggers conflict. Because you were brought up in different homes, you are likely to see the world differently. As you are both individuals with your own likes, dislikes, hopes, fears, and expectations, there will always be room for disagreement.

When a man and a woman decide to commit to each other, it's never going to be smooth sailing. There is a temptation to assume that once you've gotten past all of the awkward dating, the wrangling over cohabitating, and even the "big question," the hard work is done and you can simply put your feet up and enjoy being blissfully in love. But the basic building blocks of who we are provide a constant breeding ground for conflict. And this is healthy. After all, what would be the point of relationships if we all felt the same and could never learn anything from one another? Disagreeing with a partner is a great way of challenging his beliefs, your beliefs, and affirming the strength of your relationship—as long as this dialogue is carried out in a constructive and open way.

Being a happy couple and developing a strong relationship is all about effective communication. Just because a couple feels that sometimes Mars and Venus are just too far apart to reach a compromise doesn't mean they can't bridge this gap with a calm, rational explanation of why their feelings are so different. What they need to recognize is that much of their frustration is not the result of incompatibility. The problems don't arise just because you are a woman and he is a man. They arise because you have not learned to read each other correctly, and it is far easier to jump to false conclusions and make unjustified accusations. Clarity of communication is the first thing couples should look at when evaluating the way they interact with each other.

Challenge your ears!

In almost any interaction between couples, each will have automatic thoughts that influence what they say, how they say it, and what they do. The good news is that although these automatic thought processes and their consequent behavior are deeply ingrained, they are not completely re-sistant to change. Using a combination of techniques and effort you can break the chain between your thoughts and that automatic reaction.

When you and your partner hit a communication barrier, examine your own behavior. As you have an emotional reaction to something, try to catch the moment when you switch from feeling hurt or angry to having an inner dialogue or automatic thought. Try to match the event or the action to the thought process.

Examine your internal dialogue and learn to master your emotions and your reactions. Try to be aware of absolute lines of thinking like "He *never* listens to me. Here we go again" or "He thinks we're going to be late because I'm completely useless and disorganized."

Simply recognizing your automatic thoughts does not necessarily change them. In order to do that, determine whether your thoughts are distorted or erroneous by putting them to the test. Understand that even though your thoughts appear to be valid and true, they may not stand up to scrutiny. Ask yourself:

1. What is the evidence in favor of my interpretation?
2. What is the evidence against my interpretation?
3. Is there any alternative explanation for his or her behavior?

Through the use of logic, argument, persuasion, ridicule, or humor, an effort can be made to challenge the irrational beliefs that cause difficulties in a relationship. This requires you to be really honest with yourself. It is hard work, but the emotional benefits of learning to put your thinking errors into perspective are invaluable.

YOU ARE LEARNING TO SPEAK A NEW LANGUAGE

The ability to communicate with each other successfully is the sign of a good relationship, as we've seen through our examination of dating, sex, adultery, and everything in between. But all too often couples slip into routines of bad communication, and these are incredibly hard to escape. He sighs, you get angry, you tut, he leaves the room, you scream, he slams the door, and so on and so on. We fall into a vicious circle that feels comfortable, even if it is making both partners unhappy. Breaking that cycle and reestablishing your communication will strengthen your relationship. The good news is that really minor changes in your behavior can dramatically improve your relationship, whether you are discussing marriage, babies, or what takeout to get that evening.

When we talk about acquiring new behaviors, this doesn't mean that you and your partner have to undergo personality transplants. You are who you are, and the little personality quirks you possess are probably the reason your partner fell in love with you in the first place. More commonly, small subtle changes are required to turn your relationship around. Small changes can lead to spectacularly big results! But changes, no matter how small, are often scary. Often, the biggest fear is that we will get it wrong. It can really help to accept that mistakes are commonplace for everybody. If you are serious about changing the communication rut you and your partner have slipped into, perseverance is essential.

Keep trying. No one said it would be easy. Major relationship changes do not occur overnight. Start with realistic expectations so you don't find yourself disappointed, disillusioned, and despondent about the whole process. If you give up, your partner will feel that his efforts are underappreciated and the process is likely to fail miserably.

Changing automatic thought processes and behaviors within your relationship is a two-way process, and it is important for both partners to recognize when the other is making a concerted effort to turn things around. Even when these gestures seem small or insignificant, remember dramatic relationship improvements start with the first steps. Be positive about the progress. Acknowledge that your partner is making an effort.

Challenge your negative thoughts. As much as you should be positive about your partner's contribution, you should also be positive about your own. Stay in control of those negative thoughts that will make you feel that the situation is hopeless. Pat yourself on the back when you know you have stopped the thought-action process and actively behaved in a way that is more productive for your relationship.

IF YOU REMEMBER NOTHING ELSE!

There are fun elements in every relationship—the affection, the excitement, the tenderness. And there are the less exciting, stable elements—the security, the reassurance, and the support. After a certain amount of time together, it is fairly common to discover that the latter set of elements have the longer shelf life. Sooner or later, the number of butterflies you feel in your stomach when he calls decreases significantly. Eventually you can even manage a whole shopping trip without holding hands down every aisle. And every couple hits the realization that the bedroom has become more about sleeping than wild passion. And all of this is just the start. The infatuation period is easy. Making the relationship work is hard.

Fighting, conflict, and hurt will eventually rear their ugly heads. When couples misunderstand each other, they begin to see distorted, negative interpretations of each other and they come to expect the worst. And as we've seen, it is a rare individual who is ever aware of this misinterpretation. People just don't monitor their behavior and reactions all the time. Instead, they misread their partner's behavior, ascribe possibly imaginary motives to it, and jump to illogical conclusions. It rarely occurs to us that the way we see things is wrong or that our behavior could be based on a trigger that never existed. In a nutshell, always remember to:

1. **Examine your core beliefs and assess how realistic they are.** Avoid jumping to conclusions or assuming you have magically acquired the ability to read minds. Ask your partner what he thinks instead of telling him what you assume he thinks.

2. **Negotiate, negotiate, negotiate.** If you are having problems communicating with each other, you must assess

where you are going wrong and negotiate a solution that works for both of you. Aid the negotiation by suggesting ways you aim to contribute to the solution by changing your behavior. Do not discuss problems abstractly ("We have marital problems"). It doesn't help you nail down a solution. Focus on the specifics and it will be far easier to understand how change can be introduced.

3. Any problem is an important problem. Never underestimate what is bothering your partner. When problems are reported or identified, it is important that you actually listen to what your partner wants and encourage him to open up about any concerns he may have, big or small.

4. There may be no perfect solution. Communicate your willingness to understand that your partner sees things differently and you are more likely to reach an amicable point where you both feel secure in the relationship and where opposing views are listened to and respected.

5. Express your love and affection for your partner. When it comes to the crux of the matter, the most important feeling is mutual love. Make sure you are still affectionate with each other. Take time to kiss, cuddle, and give compliments.

6. Show sensitivity to your partner's concerns and vulnerable spots. When your partner overreacts to certain things, avoid being critical or rejecting those concerns. Gently explore what your partner's worries or fears are. Resist passing judgment, and instead view these overreactions as signs of vulnerabilities. Accept your role as a team member to help your partner work though them.

Once you get these things right, the results can be life changing. Sharing positive thoughts and behaviors is like making deposits at the bank. Over time, a healthy, robust level of credit is established and this safety net will see you and your partner through the tough times.

HAPPILY EVER AFTER—REALITY STYLE

"Happily ever after" is the most commonly used and least accurate storybook cliché in existence. Not because everlasting happiness is unattainable, but because it gives the impression that you and your partner will negotiate one initial tough battle, usually in the early stages of your relationship, and then, once you've conquered that, everything else will be smooth sailing. After you've mounted his white stallion and ridden off into the sunset, it's happy days for everyone. Yeah, right!

Truthfully, men and women will never live in perfect storybook harmony with each other because they just weren't built that way. For the same reason that you're good at discussing intricate emotional problems and he's good at reading a map, you and your man will differ dramatically in the way you see each other, your relationship, and the whole wide world. And that will never change. He will never think that "What should I do?" means "I want to mull this over for hours, make a decision, cry because it's the wrong one, and then talk about it for another six years." Equally, you will never think "I'm tired" means "I'm tired." You'll hear it as "I've lost interest in you because I'm not as attracted to you as I used to be." That's the bad news.

The good news is, with a little acceptance and a game plan for dealing with the curve balls life throws at you, you and your partner can overcome things. The advice you learned in this book won't help the two of you become the same person or cause either of you to think in exactly the same way. What it *will* do, if you have been listening properly (!), is let you realize you have your own opinions and your own experiences, and that's OK. By putting things in perspective and moderating your communication to make it compatible with your partner's, you will now be better equipped to deal with all those misunderstandings. Whenever you feel that you and your partner are speaking entirely different languages, just reassess not only what is being said but what is being heard. Then you can establish a more helpful communication structure and ensure that you and your partner are one step closer to the *real* happily ever after.

SELECTED REFERENCES

Chapter 1. When He Says "Tomato," You Hear "I Hate You"

Beck, A. T. (1964) "Thinking and Depression: II. Theory and Therapy." *Archives of General Psychiatry* 10, 561–71.

Beck, A. T., J. Rush, B. Shaw, and G. Emery (1979) *Cognitive Therapy of Depression.* New York: Guilford.

Bee, H. (1999) *The Growing Child: An Applied Approach.* New York: Longman.

Berscheid, E. (1985) "Interpersonal Attraction," in G. Lindzey and E. Aronson (eds), *Handbook of Social Psychology,* Vol. 2. New York: Random House, 413–84.

Bowlby, J. (1988) *A Secure Base.* New York: Basic Books.

Caldwell, M. A., and L. A. Peplau. (1982) "Sex Differences in Same Sex Friendship." *Sex Roles: A Journal of Research* 8(7), 721–32.

McKay, M., and P. Fanning. (1991) *Prisoners of Belief: Exposing and Changing Beliefs That Control Your Life.* Oakland, CA: New Harbinger.

Unger, R. K. (1979) *Female and Male: Psychological Perspectives.* New York: Harper & Row.

Workman, L., and W. Reader. (2004) *Evolutionary Psychology: An Introduction.* Cambridge: Cambridge University Press.

Chapter 2. Flirting and Courting

Baumeister, R. E., K. R. Catanese, and K. D. Vohs. (2001) "Is There a Gender Difference in Strength of Sex Drive? Theoretical Views, Conceptions, and a Review of Relevant Evidence." *Personality and Social Psychology Review* 5, 242–73.

Buss, D. M., and D. P. Schmidt. (1993) "Sexual Strategies Theory: An Evolutionary Perspective on Human Mating," *Psychological Review* 100, 204–32.

Cox, T. (2008) *Flirting and Body Language.* BBC.CO.UK.

Cox, T. (2003) *Superflirt.* London: Dorling Kindersley.

Lott, D. A., and F. Veronsky. (1999) "The New Flirting Game." *Psychology Today*, January/February.

Rogers, J. E. (1999) "Flirting Fascination." *Psychology Today*, January/February.

Rose, S., and I. H. Frieze. (1989) "Young Singles' Scripts for a First Date." *Gender and Society* 3, 258–68.

Unger, R. K. (1979) *Female and Male: Psychological Perspectives.* New York: Harper & Row.

Williams, J. H. (1987) *Psychology of Women: Behavior in a Biosocial Context,* 3rd ed. New York: Norton.

Chapter 3. The Fun and Frustrating First Dates

Epstein, N. B., and D. H. Baucom. (2003) *Enhanced Cognitive Behavioral Therapy for Couples: A Contextual Approach.* Washington, DC: American Psychological Association.

Feeney, J. A. (2003) "The Systemic Nature of Couple Relationships: An Attachment Perspective," in P. Erdman and T. Caffery (eds), *Attachment and Family Systems: Conceptual, Empirical and Therapeutic Relatedness*. New York: Brunner-Routledge, 139–63.

Furman, W., and A. Flanagan. (1997) "The Influence of Earlier Relationships on Marriage: An Attachment Perspective," in W. K. Halford and H. J. Markman (eds), *Clinical Handbook of Marriage and Couples Interventions*. New York: Wiley.

Hulson, B., and R. Russell. (1994) "Psychological Foundations of Couple Relationships," in D. Hooper and W. Dryden (eds), *Couple Therapy: A Handbook*. Milton Keynes, UK: Open University, 37–56.

Morr, M. C., and P. A. Mongeau. (2004) "First Date Expectations: The Impact of Sex Initiator, Alcohol Consumption, and Relationship Type." *Communication Research* 31 (1), 3–35.

Pervin, L. A., and O. P. John. (2001) *Personality: Theory and Research*, 8th ed. New York: Wiley.

Shotland, R. L., and J. M. Craig. (1988) "Can Men and Women Differentiate Between Friendly and Sexually Interested Behaviour?" *Social Psychology Quarterly* 51(1), 66–73.

Chapter 4. Welcome to Coupledom

Ainsworth, M. D. S., M. C. Blehar, E. Waters, and S. Wall. (1978) *Patterns of Attachment: A Psychological Study of the Strange Situation*. Hillsdale, NJ: Erlbaum.

Bowlby, J. (1980) *Loss: Sadness and Depression* in Attachment and Loss Series, Vol. 3. New York: Basic.

Butler, G., and C. Surawy. (2004) "Avoidance of Affect," in J. Bennett Levy, G. Butler, M. Fennell, A. Hackmann, M. Mueller, and D. Westbrook (eds), *Oxford Guide to Behavioural Experiments in Cognitive Therapy*. Oxford: Oxford University Press.

Padesky, C. A. (1994) "Schema Change Processes in Cognitive Therapy." *Clinical Psychology and Psychotherapy* 1(5), 267–78.

Shaver, P., and C. Hazan. (1988) "A Biased Overview of the Study of Love." *Journal of Social and Personal Relationships* 5, 473–501.

Shaver, P., C. Hazan, and D. Bradshaw. (1988) "Love as Attachment: The Integration of Three Behavioral Systems," in R. F. Sternberg and M. L. Barnes (eds), *The Psychology of Love*. New Haven: Yale University Press.

Simpson, J. A., W. S. Rholes, and J. S. Nelligan. (1992) "Support Seeking and Support Giving Within Couples in an Anxiety Provoking Situation: The Role of Attachment Styles." *Journal of Personality and Social Psychology* 62, 434–46.

Street, E. (1994) "Couple Therapy in the Family Context," in D. Hooper and W. Dryden (eds), *Couple Therapy: A Handbook*. Milton Keynes, UK: Open University, 12–36.

Williams, S., J. Connolly, and Z. V. Segal. (2001) "Intimacy in Relationships and Cognitive Vulnerability to Depression in Adolescent Girls." *Cognitive Therapy and Research* 25 (4), 477–96.

Young, J. E., J. S. Klosko, and M. Weishaar. (2003) *Schema Therapy: A Practitioner's Guide.* New York: Guilford.

Chapter 5. Let's Talk About Sex, Baby

Alexander, M. G., and T. D. Fisher. (2003) "Truth and Consequences: Using the Bogus Pipeline to Examine Sex Differences in Self-Reported Sexuality." *Journal of Sex Research* 40(1), 27–35.

Byers, E. S. (1996) "How Well Does the Traditional Sexual Script Explain Sexual Coercion? Review of a Program Research," *Journal of Psychology and Human Sexuality* 8, 7–25.

Carlson, N. R. (1998) *Physiology of Behavior.* Boston: Allyn and Bacon.

Cupach, W. R., and S. Metts. (1991) "Sexuality and Communication in Close Relationships," in L. McKinney and S. Sprecher (eds), *Sexuality in Close Relationships.* Hillsdale, NJ: Erlbaum.

DeLameter, J. (1987) "Gender Differences in Sexual Scenarios," in K. Kelley (ed.), *Females, Males, and Sexuality: Theories and Research.* Albany, NY: State University of New York, 127–39.

Ferroni, P., and J. Taffee. (1997) "Women's Emotional Well-Being: The Importance of Communicating Sexual Needs." *Sexual and Marital Therapy* 12, 127–38.

Ford, V. (2005) *Overcoming Sexual Problems: A Self Help Guide Using Cognitive Behavioral Techniques.* London: Robinson.

Haavio-Mannila, E., O. Kontula, and A. Rotkirch. (2002) *Sexual Lifestyles in the Twentieth Century: A Research Study.* New York: Palgrave.

Herold, E. S., and L. Way. (1988) "Sexual Self-Disclosure Among University Women." *Journal of Sex Research* 24, 1–14.

Joffe, H., and A. C. Franca-Koh. (2001) "Parental Non-Verbal Sexual Communication: Its Relationship to Sexual Behaviour and Sexual Guilt." *Journal of Health Psychology* 6 (1), 17–30.

Leiblum, S. R. (2002) "Reconsidering Gender Differences in Sexual Desire: An Update." *Sexual and Relationship Therapy* 17, 57–68.

Ofman, U. (2000) Guest editor's note, *Journal of Sex Education and Therapy* 25, 3–5.

Pick, S., and P. A. Palos. (1995) "Impact of the Family on the Sex Lives of Adolescents." *Adolescence* 30, 667–75.

Simm, W., and J. H. Gagnon. (1986) "Sexual Scripts: Performance and Change." *Archives of Sexual Behaviour* 15(2), 97–120.

Chapter 6. Confronting Commitment Issues

Baucom, D. H., N. Epstein, S. L. Sayers, and T. G. Sher. (1989) "The Role of Cognitions in Marital Relationships: Definitional, Methodological, and Conceptual Issues." *Journal of Consulting and Clinical Psychology* 57, 31–8.

Collard, J., and P. Mansfield. (1994) "The Couple: A Sociological Perspective," in D. Hooper and W. Dryden (eds), *Couple Therapy: A Handbook.* Milton Keynes, UK: Open University, 12–36.

Crowe, M. (2005) *Overcoming Relationship Problems: A Self-Help Guide Using Cognitive Behavioral Techniques.* London: Robinson.

Leahy, R. L. (2003) *Cognitive Therapy Techniques: A Practitioner's Guide.* New York: Guilford.

Lefrancois, G. (1990) *The Lifespan,* 3rd ed. Belmont, CA: Wadsworth.

Lewis, J. (2001) *The End of Marriage? Individualism and Intimate Relations.* Cheltenham, UK: Edward Elgar.

Rindfuss, R. R., and A. VandenHeuvel. (1990) "Cohabitation: A Precursor to Marriage or an Alternative to Being Single?" *Population and Development Review* 16 (4), 703–26.

Chapter 7. Meeting the In-Laws

Apter, D. T. (1999) British Psychological Society's conference. BBC News, December 21, 1999, "The Real Trouble with In-Laws," http://news.bbc.co.uk/1/hi/uk/573446.stm.

Flecknoe, P., and D. Sanders. (2004) "Interpersonal Difficulties," in J. Bennett-Levy, G. Butler, M. Fennell, A. Hackmann, M. Mueller, and D. Westbrook (eds), *Oxford Guide to Behavioural Experiments in Cognitive Therapy.* Oxford: Oxford University Press, 393–409.

McCarthy, B., and E. McCarthy. (2004) *Getting It Right the First Time: Creating a Healthy Marriage,* New York: Brunner-Routledge.

McGoldrick, M. (1980) "The Joining of Families Through Marriage: The New Couple," in E. A. Carter and M. McGoldrick (eds), *The Family Life Cycle: A Framework for Family Therapy.* New York: Gardner, 93–119.

Safran, J. D., and Z. V. Segal. (1990) *Interpersonal Process in Cognitive Therapy.* New York: Basic Books.

Scott, E. (2006) "Stress Management. Top 10 Worst Ways to Handle Conflict." www.stressabout.com/b/2006/03/07.

Shucksmith, J., L. Hendry, J. Love, and T. Glendinning. (1993) "The Importance of Friendship." *Research in Education* 52, 1–5.

Chapter 8. Moving in Together

Collins, N. L., and S. J. Read. (1990) "Adult Attachment, Working Models and Relationship Quality in Dating Couples." *Journal of Personality and Social Psychology* 58, 644–63.

Crowe, M. (2005) *Overcoming Relationship Problems: A Self-Help Guide Using Cognitive Behavioral Techniques.* London: Robinson.

Epstein, N. B., and D. H. Baucom. (2003) *Enhanced Cognitive Behavioral Therapy for Couples: A Contextual Approach*. Washington, DC: American Psychological Association.

Hewstone, M., and W. Stroebe (eds). (2007) *Introduction to Social Psychology*. Oxford: Blackwell.

Mayer, J. D., and P. Salovey. (1993) "The Intelligence of Emotional Intelligence," *Intelligence* 17, 433–42.

McGoldrick, M. (1980) "The Joining of Families Through Marriage: The New Couple," in E. A. Carter and M. McGoldrick (eds), *The Family Life Cycle: A Framework for Family Therapy*. New York: Gardner, 93–119.

Prinz, C. (1995) *Cohabiting, Married, or Single*. Hants, UK: Avebury.

Thomson, E., and U. Colella. (1992) "Cohabitation and Marital Stability: Quality or Commitment?" *Journal of Marriage and the Family* 54, 259–67.

Chapter 9. Fighting Fair

Beck, A. T. (1988) *Love Is Never Enough*. New York: Harper Perennial.

Baucom, D. H., and N. Epstein. (1990) *Cognitive Behavioral Marital Therapy*. New York: Brunner/Mazel.

Hall, P. (2007) BBC Home Web page: "Relationships: How to Argue." July.

Heaton, T. B., and A. M. Blake. (1999) "Gender Differences in Determinants of Marital Disruption," *Journal of Family Issues* 20 (1), 25–45.

Crowe, M. (2005) *Overcoming Relationship Problems: A Self-Help Guide Using Cognitive Behavioral Techniques.* London: Robinson.

Padesky, C., and D. Greenberger. (1995) *Mind Over Mood.* Palo Alto, CA: Guilford.

Quilliam, S. (2001) *The 10 Point Plan for Couples in Conflict.* London: Vermillion.

Chapter 10. When He (or You) Cheats

Atwater, L. (1982) *The Extramarital Connection.* New York: Irvington.

Bailey, J. M., S. Gaulin, Y. Agyei, and B. A. Gladue. (1994) "Effects of Gender and Sexual Orientation on Evolutionary Relevant Aspects of Human Mating." *Journal of Personality and Social Psychology* 66, 1081–93.

Baumeister, R. E, K. R. Catanese, and K. D. Vohs. (2001) "Is There a Gender Difference in Strength of Sex Drive? Theoretical Views, Conceptual Distinctions, and a Review of Relevant Evidence." *Personality and Social Psychology Review* 5, 242–73.

Betzig, L. (1989) "Causes of Conjugal Dissolution: A Cross-Study." *Current Anthropology* 30, 654–76.

Brown, E. M. (2001) *Patterns of Infidelity and Their Treatment.* Philadelphia: Brunner-Routledge.

Buunk, B. P., and P. Dijkstra. (2004) "Gender Differences in Rival Characteristics That Evoke Jealousy in Response to Emotional Versus Sexual Infidelity." *Personal Relationships* 11, 395–408.

Buunk, B. P., and B. van Driel. (1989) *Variant Lifestyles and Relationships.* London: Sage.

Buus, D. M., and T. K. Shackelford. (1997) "Susceptibility to Infidelity in the First Year of Marriage." *Journal of Research in Personality* 31, 193–221.

Buus, D. M., R. J. Larsen, D. Westen, and J. Semmelroth. (1992) "Sex Differences in Jealousy: Evolution, Physiology and Psychology." *Psychological Science* 3, 251–55.

Buus, D. M., T. K. Shackelford, J. Choe, P. Dijkstra, and B. P. Buunk. (2000) "Distress about Mating Rivals." *Personal Relationships* 7, 235–43.

Carnes, P. (1983) *Out of the Shadows.* Minneapolis, MN: CompCare.

DeSteno, D. A., and P. Salovey. (1996) "Jealousy and the Characteristics of One's Rival: A Self-Evaluation Maintenance Perspective." *Personality and Social Psychology Bulletin* 22, 920–32.

Epstein, N. B., and D. H. Baucom. (2003) *Enhance Cognitive Behavioral Therapy for Couples: A Contextual Approach.* Washington, DC: American Psychological Association.

Glass, S. P., and T. L. Wright. (1985) "Sex Differences in Type of Extramarital Involvement and Marital Dissatisfaction." *Sex Roles* 12, 1102–20.

Goodall, J. (1986) "Justifications for Extramarital Relationships: The Association Between Attitudes, Behaviors and Gender." *Journal of Sex Research* 29, 361–87.

Hayman, S. (2001) *Moving On: Breaking Up Without Breaking Down.* London: Vermillion.

Lawson, A. (1988) *Adultery: An Analysis of Love and Betrayal.* New York: Basic.

Leahy, R. L. (2003) *Cognitive Therapy Techniques: A Practitioner's Guide.* New York: Guilford.

Murphy, A., R. Vallacher, T. Shackelford, D. Bjorklund, and J. Yunger. (2005) *Relationship Experience as a Predictor of Romantic Jealousy.* Florida Atlantic University, Department of Psychology.

Okami, P., and T. K. Shackelford. (2001) "Human Sex Differences in Sexual Psychology and Behavior." *Annual Review of Sex Research* 12, 186–241.

Spanier, G. B., and R. L. Margolis. (1983) "Marital Separation and Extramarital Sexual Behaviour." *Journal of Sex Research* 19, 23–48.

Chapter 11. We Need to Talk

Beal, E. (1980) "Separation, Divorce and Single Parent Families," in E. A. Carter and M. McGoldrick (eds), *The Family Life Cycle: A Framework for Family Therapy*. New York: Gardner, 241–64.

Beck, A. T. (1988) *Love Is Never Enough*. New York: Harper & Row.

Bennett-Levy, J., G. Butler, M. Fennell, A. Hackmann, M. Mueller, and D. Westbrook (eds), *Oxford Guide to Behavioural Experiments in Cognitive Therapy*. Oxford: Oxford University Press.

Bourne, E. J. (2005) *The Anxiety and Phobia Workbook*, 4th ed. New York: New Harbinger.

Christensen, A., and C. L. Heavey. (1990) "Gender and Social Structure in the Demand/Withdraw Pattern of Marital Conflict." *Journal of Personality and Social Psychology* 59, 73–81.

Crowe, M. (2005) *Overcoming Relationship Problems: A Self-Help Guide Using Cognitive Behavioral Techniques*. London: Robinson.

Duck, S. (2005) "How Do You Tell Someone You're Letting Go?" *The Psychologist* 18(4), 210–13.

Epstein, N. B., and D. H. Baucom. (2003) *Enhanced Cognitive Behavioral Therapy for Couples: A Contextual Approach*. Washington, DC: American Psychological Association.

Flecknoe, P., and D. Sanders. (2001) "Interpersonal Difficulties," in S. Hayman (ed), *Moving On: Breaking Up Without Breaking Down*. London: Vermillion.

Jordan, M., C. Proot, C. Fleming, and M. Jernigan. (2002) "Methods to End Relationships: Typical Behaviors and Statements Used to End a Romantic Relationship," paper presented at the annual convention of the American Psychological Society, New Orleans, 2002.

Jordan, M., M. Shriner, C. Proot, K. Bledsoe, and A. Mahoney. (2002) "Six Dimensions of the Breakup of Romantic Relationships," paper presented at the annual convention of the American Psychological Society, New Orleans, 2002.

Leahy, R. L. (2003) *Cognitive Therapy Techniques: A Practitioner's Guide*. New York: Guilford.

Safran, J. D., and Z. V. Segal. (1990) *Interpersonal Process in Cognitive Therapy*. New York: Basic.

Sayers, S. L., C. S. Kohn, D. M. Fresco, A. S. Bellack, and D. B. Sarwer. (2001) "Marital Cognitions and Depression in the Context of Marital Discord." *Cognitive Therapy and Research* 25(6), 713–32.

Vanzetti, N. A., C. I. Notarious, and D. NeeSmith. (1992) "Specific and Generalised Expectancies in Marital Interaction." *Journal of Family Psychology* 6, 171–83.

Wachtel, E. (1999) *We Love Each Other but . . . : Simple Secrets to Strengthen Your Relationship and Make Love Last*, New York: St. Martin's Griffin.

Williams, J. H. (1987) *Psychology of Women: Behavior in a Biosocial Context,* 3rd ed. New York: Norton.

Chapter 12. Marriage Material

Berger, P., and H. Kellner. (1964) "Marriage and the Construction of Reality." *Diogenes* 49–72.

Collard, J., and P. Mansfield. (1994) "The Couple: A Sociological Perspective," in D. Hooper and W. Dryden (eds), *Couple Therapy: A Handbook.* Milton Keynes, UK: Open University, 12–36.

Dafoe Whitehead, B., and D. Popenoe. (2006) "State of Our Unions," annual assessment for the National Marriage Project at Rutgers, the State University of New Jersey.

Erber, R., and R. Gilmour. (1994) "Courtship Antecedents of Marital Satisfaction and Love," in R. Erber and R. Gilmour (eds), *Theoretical Perspectives on Personal Relationships.* Hillsdale, NJ: Erlbaum, 43–65.

Haley, J. (1963) "Marriage Therapy." *Archives of General Psychiatry* 8, 213–34.

Halford, W. K., A. Kelly, and H. J. Markman (1997) "The Concept of Healthy Marriage," in W. K. Halford and H. J. Markman (eds), *Clinical Handbook of Marriage and Couples Interventions.* West Sussex, UK: Wiley, 3–12.

Horwitz, A. V., H. R. White, and S. Howell White. (1996) "Becoming Married and Mental Health: A Longitudinal Study of a Cohort of Young Adults." *Journal of Marriage and the Family* 58(4), 895–907.

Mansfield, P., and J. Collard. (1988) *The Beginning of the Rest of Your Life?* London: Palgrave Macmillan.

McCarthy, B., and E. McCarthy. (2004) *Getting It Right the First Time: Creating a Healthy Marriage.* New York: Brunner-Routledge.

McGoldrick, M. (1980) "The Joining of Families Through Marriage: The New Couple," in E. A. Carter and M. McGoldrick (eds), *The Family Life Cycle: A Framework for Family Therapy.* New York: Gardner, 93–119.

Unger, R. K. (1979) *Female and Male: Psychological Perspectives.* New York: Harper & Row.

Chapter 13. A Real Life Happily Ever After

Beck, A. T. (1967). *Depression: Clinical, Experimental, and Theoretical Aspects.* New York: Harper & Row.

Crowe, M. (2005) *Overcoming Relationship Problems: A Self-Help Guide Using Cognitive Behavioral Techniques.* London: Robinson.

Dindia, K., M. A. Fitzpatrick, and D. A. Kenny. (1989) *Self-Disclosure in Spouse and Stranger Dyads: A Social Relations Analysis.* San Francisco: International Communication Associations.

Epstein, N. B., and D. H. Baucom. (2003) *Enhanced Cognitive Behavioral Therapy for Couples: A Contextual Approach.* Washington, DC: American Psychological Association.

Halford, W. K., A. Kelly, and H. J. Markman. (1997) "The Concept of a Healthy Marriage," in K. W. Halford and H. J. Markman (eds), *Clinical Handbook of Marriage and Couples Interventions*, West Sussex, UK: Wiley, 3–12.

Leahy, R. L. (2003) *Cognitive Therapy Techniques: A Practitioner's Guide.* New York: Guilford.

Padesky, C., and D. Greenberger. (1995) *Mind Over Mood.* Palo Alto, CA: Guilford.

Weeks, G. R., and S. R. Treat. (2005) *Couples in Treatment: Techniques and Approaches for Practice.* Philadelphia, PA: Brunner-Routledge.